OUTSOURCING

AND

HUMAN

RESOURCES

Trends, Models, and Guidelines

OUTSOURCING
AND
HUMAN
RESOURCES

Trends, Models, and Guidelines

Philip J. Harkins

Stephen M. Brown

Russell Sullivan

LER
PRESS

Published by
LER Press
110 Hartwell Avenue
Lexington, Massachusetts 02173
617-862-3157

Library of Congress Catalog Card Number: 96-75627

ISBN 0-9651470-0-2

First Printing 1996
Printed in the United States of America

Table of Contents

Figure Index

Introduction

What should you outsource? Why should you outsource? How should you outsource? This book discusses these and other critical issues involved in outsourcing within the human resources context. In so doing, the book provides a context for understanding outsourcing, models to implement outsourcing, and specific skill chapters on how to outsource.

For the purposes of this book, "outsourcing" means "having an external vendor provide, on a recurring basis, a service that would normally be performed within the organization." But don't be misled by this definition or by the book's title (*Outsourcing and Human Resources*). This book is not simply about "outsourcing." Clearly, the principles that underlie outsourcing apply to other types of strategic partnerships, as well. In the shrink and drive business mode of the 1990s, HR professionals are entering, building, and mastering an array of strategic alliances that improve performance and cut costs. While we do not advocate outsourcing or any strategic partnership *per se*, this book will help you gain knowledge and present facts to your organization around the subject of outsourcing and strategic partnerships.

Nor is this book merely about "human resources," at least in the traditional sense. For sure, much of this book is directed at the outsourcing of traditional human resource services and functions. Other parts of the book, however, discuss outsourcing in a broader sense, *e.g.*, what impact HR professionals can have *organizationally* through outsourcing. Moreover, many of the models and guidelines contained herein have general application to other areas or functions of business that are also grappling with the issues presented by outsourcing and strategic partnerships. In fact, many of these models and guidelines were derived in part from the experiences that individuals in information systems, manufacturing, marketing, and other segments of the "non-HR world" have had with outsourcing. Because of these intersections between HR and other functional areas, we expect that leaders in those other functional areas will also have much to gain by reading this book.

This book is nevertheless targeted at human resource leaders who are interested in learning more about outsourcing. The primary purpose of this book is, in fact, to provide human resource professionals with the information, knowledge, and tools that they need to become the internal organizational expert on outsourcing. It contains a healthy mixture of theory and practice, with an emphasis on the practical.

The book has ten chapters divided into three parts. Part One ("Trends") contains a collection of views and data that attempts to make sense of the outsourcing phenomenon within human resources — both in the present and in the future. Part Two ("Models") features an approach toward outsourcing (as well as an alternative approach to outsourcing) that you can employ in guiding your entry into this new world of strategic partnerships. Finally, Part Three ("Guidelines") provides a set of practical guidelines directed at the implementation stage — that is, how to outsource. The book concludes with some Bibliographic Notes that direct the reader to further literature and resources (both within HR and in general) on the subject of each of the ten chapters.

When we decided to write this book, we chose to include the viewpoints of other outsourcing strategists and industry leaders in order to provide the reader with a wide spectrum of voices on the subject. This book has five contributing authors — namely, Merrill Anderson of NCR Worldwide Services, Gary Breitbart of Alexander & Alexander Consulting Group, Dennis Colling of Partners HealthCare System, Jac Fitz-enz of Saratoga Institute, and Reed Keller of Coopers & Lybrand. Where one of these contributing authors wrote a chapter, his byline appears under the chapter heading accordingly.

We are glad that we decided to capture a multitude of voices in this book, because the rapidly changing human resources world is growing in different directions, requiring input from different viewpoints. Much of this change concerns outsourcing and strategic partnerships. It is our hope that this book will help the HR professional understand this change and, ultimately, master it.

Authors

PHILIP J. HARKINS is President and CEO of Linkage, Incorporated, an international organizational development and corporate education company headquartered in Lexington, Massachusetts. Dr. Harkins has consulted to numerous *Fortune 500* companies worldwide on a host of human resource, organizational development, strategic, and corporate education issues. Prior to founding Linkage in 1988, he held senior management positions at Raytheon, Keane, Inc., and Boston University. A trainer, consultant, and authority on organizational development, Dr. Harkins has authored a number of publications on a wide variety of organizational development issues. He graduated from Merrimack College and received his doctorate from Harvard University.

STEPHEN M. BROWN is Dean of the Center for Adult Learning and Associate Professor of management and education at Lesley College in Cambridge, Massachusetts. Dr. Brown previously served as the Dean of the Graduate School and School of Management at Lesley College. He has consulted to numerous organizations, governmental agencies, and universities on a host of corporate education and organizational development issues. Dr. Brown is the author of numerous articles and a frequent conference speaker. He received his doctorate from Boston University, a Master's degree from the University of Rhode Island, and a bachelor's degree from UMass-Dartmouth.

RUSSELL SULLIVAN is a consultant and counsel for Linkage, Inc. In his consulting work, he is the practice leader at Linkage for outsourcing and strategic partnerships. Prior to joining Linkage, Mr. Sullivan was a litigation associate for the Washington, D.C. law firm of Wiley, Rein & Fielding. The author of several articles on organizational development and legal issues, he is a graduate of Yale University and Harvard Law School.

Contributing Authors

MERRILL C. ANDERSON has over 14 years experience in designing and implementing organizational change efforts for *Fortune 500* companies. He is currently the Vice President of Organization Development for NCR Worldwide Services in Dayton, Ohio. Prior to joining NCR, Dr. Anderson was the Director of Organization Capability Services for Amoco Corporation in Chicago. An adjunct Professor in Organization Development at Illinois Benedictine College, Dr. Anderson has a Ph.D. in psychology from New York University, a M.A. from the University of Toronto, and a B.A. from the University of Colorado.

GARY L. BREITBART is the Director of Information Technologies for Alexander & Alexander Consulting Group, Inc., a human resource management consulting firm headquartered in Lyndhurst, New Jersey. In his current position, Mr. Breitbart is responsible for the planning, marketing, and product develop-ment/management functions of the practice. He has designed, developed, and implemented numerous human resource and employee benefits systems. As well, he has assisted many clients in framing their outsourcing strategies and in developing busi-ness cases to drive outsourcing decisions. Mr. Breitbart received a Master's of Business Administration from the Harvard Busi-ness School, a Master's degree in Interactive Telecommunications from New York University, and a B.S. in Economics from Uni-versity of Pennsylvania's Wharton School.

DENNIS COLLING serves as Vice President for Partners HealthCare System, Inc. in Boston, Massachusetts. His primary responsibili-ties include Human Resources Management and Organizational Effectiveness for the integrated health care system founded by the Brigham and Women's Hospital and the Massachusetts General Hospital. The System includes Partners Community HealthCare, Inc., a network of community providers, and a grow-ing number of owned and affiliated practices and institutions. Mr. Colling previously served as Associate Vice President of the

University of Pennsylvania Health System, where he was responsible for strategic human resources management. For nine years he served as the Human Resources and Information Systems executive at the Catherine McAuley Health System in Ann Arbor, Michigan. Mr. Colling holds an A.B. in Political Science and an M.B.A. from the University of Michigan.

JAC FITZ-ENZ is founder and President of Saratoga Institute in Santa Clara, California, a consulting firm specializing in performance measurement and improvement. He is the father of staff benchmarking and performance evaluation and one of the pioneers in improving the financial value of the human resources function. Dr. Fitz-enz has written three books: *How To Measure Human Resource Management* (1984), *Human Value Management* (1990) (which won the SHRM Book of the Year Award), and *Benchmarking Staff Performance* (1993). Prior to founding Saratoga Institute in 1977, he had 20 years of business experience in several line functions and held human resource vice president positions at Wells Fargo Bank, Imperial Bank, and Motorola Computer Systems.

REED A. KELLER is a Vice Chairman of Coopers & Lybrand L.L.P. in New York City, where he is responsible for the firm's Human Resource Advisory Group and serves as a member of the firm's Management Committee. He was appointed Vice Chairman in 1992 after serving as the managing partner of the Atlantic region. Mr. Keller has consulted with management and boards of directors on a broad range of human resource management issues and is an authority on the design and administration of executive compensation programs. Prior to joining Coopers & Lybrand, Mr. Keller held various management positions at Eastman Kodak and other companies. A native Tennessean, Mr. Keller has an M.B.A. from the University of Tennessee.

Acknowledgments

The authors wish to thank the five individuals — Merrill Anderson, Gary Breitbart, Dennis Colling, Jac Fitz-enz, and Reed Keller — who each contributed a chapter to this book. In addition, we would like to thank the other industry leaders who granted us interviews and generously shared their time and insights: Julie Anixter of Anixter Inc., Cathy Falzareno of Builders Square, Ross Grossman of Prudential Insurance Company of America, June Jones of First Interstate Bancorp, and Jane Michel of Chevron Corporation.

We would also like to thank the reference librarians and staff of the following libraries for the assistance that they provided us in researching this book: Harvard Business School's Baker Library, Harvard University's Widener Library, the Boston Public Library, the Lesley College Library, Northeastern University's Snell Library, and, especially, Boston College's O'Neill Library.

We received considerable help in writing, editing, and producing this book, primarily from individuals associated with Linkage, Inc. Larry Carr was the business manager for the book, making many of the key decisions necessary for publication. In addition, he helped refine the scope of the book and contributed some insightful edits to Chapter Eight. Todd Langton was an advocate for the book from the beginning and throughout. He also played a critical conceptual role in its formation and added some excellent input to Chapter Seven. Kelly Meehan helped form the conceptual framework for the book and proved to be an invaluable resource with respect to the literature on outsourcing, as well as potential outside contributors. In addition, she contributed to the creation and development of Chapter Two.

Thanks also to David Giber for helping hone our thinking, especially with respect to Chapters One and Five. His edits and contributions were essential to the development of those chapters.

Many others added their talents to this book. While we may not have the space to detail each individual contribution, we thank all of the following for their efforts: Tom Dimieri, Teresa

Giangregorio, Laura Gerhardt, Taavo Godtfredsen, Paul Thomas Hauh, Christine Henckler, Christine Kaye, Robin Lesses, Rachel Mirovich, Jill Pelavin, Amy Perler, Dana Rigali, Ellen Rosenberg, Rich Rosier, Martha Saillant-Brown, Gretchen Shubrooks, and Theresa Thornton. All had a hand in proofreading, editing, and/or producing this book.

In addition, special thanks to Laura Krotky, Russ and Judy Sullivan, Scott Sullivan (who does all the intangibles), Kathy, Jonathan, and Jared Brown, Matt, Chris, and John Harkins, and Michele Bouchard for their patience, understanding, and encouragement. Thanks also to Tim Schroer ("Mr. Prognosis Negative") for his wit and wisdom.

Thanks also to Ilene Horowitz, our production editor from Font & Center Press in Weston, Massachusetts. Her guidance and skill in the design and coordination ensured that this entire project ran smoothly.

In the end, this book is largely the result of two individuals. Kristine Rainge played a crucial role in project coordination, helping to design the text and cover, taking care of all the small but significant details, and editing and proofreading all of the copy. And last, but certainly not least, Gina Willard was the most important person in the production of this book, inputting, proofreading, adding crucial contributions to the design of the book, and keeping everything straight and in order. Without her tireless efforts, this book would not have been possible.

Philip J. Harkins
Russell Sullivan
Lexington, Massachusetts

Stephen M. Brown
Cambridge, Massachusetts

PART ONE

TRENDS

Outsourcing has swept every segment of industry in the 1990s. What does this development mean for the human resource professional? What challenges and opportunities does outsourcing present? How widespread and pervasive is the phenomenon — and is it, in fact, a phenomenon? In what context should the HR professional place outsourcing? And how is it likely to evolve in the future?

This part of the book attempts to answer these questions and provide a context for understanding outsourcing. In Chapter One, we examine the realities of outsourcing and then analyze the challenges and opportunities that outsourcing presents for the HR professional on a strategic, organization-wide basis. Then, in Chapter Two, we present and analyze data that we have collected on outsourcing within the human resources context, thereby providing some valuable insights on what is happening in the field today. In Chapter Three, Reed Keller of Coopers & Lybrand examines how outsourcing relates and fits into the enterprise value chain. Finally, in Chapter Four, Gary Breitbart of Alexander & Alexander Consulting Group analyzes the market dynamics and predicts how HR outsourcing is likely to evolve in the future.

Chapter One

Outsourcing:

A World of Challenge and Opportunity for Human Resources

Over the past decade, the perceived importance of people has grown, while in ironic contrast, the perceived importance of the human resource function has not grown. This represents a source of frustration for human resources professionals.

The last decade has seen a profound shift in the recognition of employees as assets. While CEOs have long wanted to stock their organization with talented employees, until recently, an exceptional few saw a direct connection between the people of an organization and its bottom line. The structure, the design, the product, the service — those were the things that held the key to profit and shareholder satisfaction. In this era of globalization, shifting markets, rapid technological change and advancement, and unpredictable turbulence, most now recognize — correctly — that people are critical to attaining and sustaining what Michael Porter has termed "competitive advantage."[1] Only with people who have superior and adaptable skills, knowledge, and competencies can an organization survive the unpredictable winds of change and steer a steady course towards organizational success.

But while *humans* are now valued more than ever, the *human resources* function is not. The last decade has been, in many ways, cruel to the HR function. Many CEOs still view the HR function with a jaundiced eye: they know that they are getting *some* value from the HR function, but at the same time, they are often unclear as to exactly what they are getting — or, worse, clear about what they are getting but skeptical of its importance. Thus, when it comes to strategy and the things that really matter, human resources resembles a "B list" dinner party guest: sometimes they are invited to the table, other times they are not.

Human resource leaders aren't naive. They know that this is the way they are perceived, and they don't like it. A certain insecurity persists in the HR profession. Many HR leaders struggle to prove their worth to their organization, to show that the things they do truly matter. In fact, many HR professionals are critical to their organization's success — in the tasks and functions they perform and in the leadership they provide. They just aren't always seen in that light — and, in this case, image is reality. So the insecurity persists, and the HR leader continues to seek validation and acceptance. Despite the newly and universally recognized link between people and competitive advantage, the "people function" — human resources — finds itself at a crossroads in the mid-1990s.

As Allan Mohrman and Ed Lawler have recognized, the history of the HR function "has been one of gradual evolution and increased sophistication." With each passing decade in this century, human resources has been presented with new challenges and increased responsibilities, necessitating a continual redefinition of the role of HR. Early in the century, human resources was the "personnel department," charged with the largely bureaucratic tasks of keeping accurate employment and payroll records. The role expanded in the 1930s and 1940s with the rise of the labor movement and the need for a part of the organization to fight and deal with the unions. The sophisticated discrimination legislation of the 1960s brought on further responsibilities.[2] Thus, by the early 1970s, the function was often known as the "industrial relations" or the "employee relations" department. Later, with an ever-increasing amount of roles and responsibilities, it became "personnel relations" and then, finally, "human resources." Today, as Mohrman and Lawler point out, "human resource departments can play a major constructive role in making organizations more effective . . . For the first time in many corporations, human resource managers are being asked to participate in major business decisions."[3] To a significant extent, things have never been better for human resources.

The changing name of human resources does not mean, however, that many senior executives who began careers in the 1970s have changed their perception. As we move toward the next century, it is clear what human resources wants to be: a full-fledged strategic business partner within the organization. To attain that status, human resources must add definite and measurable value to the organization. Applying Porter's teachings, this means that HR should help its organization attain competitive advantage by differentiating its products or services through its people. In most cases, human resources does perform such a role.

But to attain the status of strategic business partner, human resources must not only add value, but also must *appear* to add value. It is clear that, in many instances, HR is not seen as adding such value, regardless of its actual value-added contributions, and is thus not seen as a full-fledged strategic business partner within the organization. Thus, in the mid-1990s, most HR leaders find themselves striving to attain the elevated status of strategic business partner. Outsourcing is the vehicle — the actual and visible vehicle — that can take them there.

The Reality of Outsourcing

Outsourcing is hardly a new concept. It is only recently, however, that the HR world has begun to pay attention to outsourcing — in large part because an increasing number of HR professionals are outsourcing HR services and functions to improve the quality and efficiency of their own HR departments or to obtain expertise in an ever more complex environment. Most of the chapters in this book examine the whens, whys, and hows of outsourcing HR services — crucial issues, indeed, to the success of your HR department in the 1990s. That is not the focus here. Instead, this chapter takes a broader perspective, focusing on what the reality of outsourcing on a grand, company-wide scale means for the HR professional.

And outsourcing is a reality. Narrowly defined, outsourcing means having an external vendor provide, on a recurring basis, a service that would normally be performed within the organization. While this is a convenient short-hand definition, the concept of "outsourcing" clearly captures a broader range of strategic partnerships. Think of it as a continuum that contains discrete relationships with consultants and attorneys on the one end, partnerships with outsourcing vendors involving a particular service or function in the middle, and broader arrangements such as "employee leasing," "virtual organizations," "network organizations," "boundaryless organizations," and "webs of inclusion" on the other.[4]

However broadly or narrowly defined, outsourcing is likely here to stay. A notion has emerged in some circles that outsourcing is a fad — a by-product of the downsizing and rightsizing cycle that has gripped most American industries in the 1990s. When downsizing and rightsizing fade from the scene, the reasoning goes, so will outsourcing. This is unlikely. American companies have been quietly outsourcing for years; since at least the 1950s, American companies have faced and made decisions as to what to do internally and what to contract out.[5] As Richard Jacobs has recognized, "The truth of the matter is that outsourcing has always been an integral component of corporate operations . . . Although there is nothing new about outsourcing, in recent times it has become more visible, more widespread, and more heatedly debated — particularly when a good outsourcing idea turns bad."[6]

What is also new and different today — besides the frequency and fanfare — is that organizations are now beginning to outsource functions, or parts thereof, that were previously seen as untouchable (manufacturing, research and development, etc.). There are no more sacred cows. James Brian Quinn and Frederick Hilmer have persuasively argued that an organization should focus on the internal resources that impact its core competence, where it can achieve definable preeminence and provide unique value for customers, and consider strategically outsourcing all other activities (including many traditionally considered integral) for which the organization has neither a critical strategic need nor special capabilities.[7] The logic underlying such an approach is sound, for no organization can be expected to master the full range of complex tasks in today's ever-changing business world. Moreover, many organizations seem to have embraced such a philosophy. It is indeed difficult to identify an industry where outsourcing has *not* become a pervasive practice.[8] Although there are no definitive statistics, one recent estimate indicates that 30 percent of *Fortune 1000* industrial corporations outsource more than 50 percent of their manufacturing. Although this is just a partial sampling covering only manufacturing, this amounts to between $100 billion and $250 billion per year.[9] The bottom line: outsourcing is big business.

What, then, does all this mean for HR? **First**, it means that, even if you have decided *not* to outsource any of your HR services or functions, outsourcing has and will continue to have an impact somewhere in your organization — you will not be able to ignore it, even if you want to. **Second** — and more important — the reality of outsourcing presents real challenges and real opportunities for the HR professional. Through outsourcing, human resources should transform itself to be congruent with the networked organization that all organizations will become. It is incumbent upon the HR organization, however, to implement the process properly, be successful, and model the transformed organization. Consider these simple truths:

- Outsourcing is essentially about people supply, and HR is in the people supplying business; thus, outsourcing is smack dead center in the middle of HR's primary function.

- Outsourcing is also a critical part of business strategy, and HR is looking for ways to commit to the business strategy and solidify its status as strategic business partner.

Taken together, these facts indicate that HR has both the obligation and the capabilities to lead the charge around outsourcing within the organization. To do so, HR must overcome the challenges that outsourcing creates and, mainly, seize the opportunities that outsourcing presents. The HR professional should become the outsourcing expert in his or her organization to reach or solidify his or her status as strategic business partner.

The Challenges of Outsourcing

Imagine a workplace where those that do the work for the organization are scattered worldwide, housed in five, ten, or twenty different facilities; where many (or most) of those who do your work aren't even your own employees; and where it is no longer possible to set your cultural identity through the summer picnic or the annual holiday party (because many of your "workers" would be physically and geographically unable to attend).

Welcome to the world of outsourcing. It is a world that is a reality now and will become even more of a reality in the future — if you think that the last ten years have witnessed great change in this direction, wait for the next ten year ride. It is a world that presents enormous challenges for the human resources function.

These challenges can be met and overcome with foresight, effort, and nuts-and-bolts programs, practices, and innovations — not with theory, and not with simple policies and procedures. The "personnel department" of yesteryear may have been able to devise and fall back upon policies and procedures, but the human resources function of today cannot, particularly when it comes to outsourcing. It is impossible to think "competitive advantage" and "strategic business partner" when you have to work in full regalia to police policies and procedures. The objective in meeting outsourcing's challenges is to have as few policies and procedures as the organization demands and, instead, to create programs, practices, and innovations that will place more of the responsibility where it belongs — the line — with human resources serving as the performance consultant and providing HR expertise.

But it all starts with human resources. The challenge that outsourcing presents for the HR leader is to create flexible, and effective programs, practices, and innovations that will guide line managers along four different dimensions: vision, workflow, competence, and systems. *See* Figure 1.1.

Vision. At any point in time, a critical question for an organization is, "Where are we going?" As a strategic business partner, human resources should help answer that question. Before it even gets to that question, however, the organization must first ask, "Who are we?" And that is a question that human resources — the function that has traditionally led the way in defining the identity and culture of an organization — must take prime responsibility in answering. In this era of outsourcing, this is easier said than done. Not too long ago, workers naturally thought of themselves as "Ford men" or "Ford women"; HR needed only feed and nourish this sense of identity to benefit the organization. In this new world, however, he or she who sits beside you may not even draw a paycheck from Ford but may, in fact, work in the Ford plant on a leased or contingent basis; other "Ford men" and "Ford women" may sit in a facility halfway across the country — or the world — and work for Ford as vendor or service provider. It is up to human resources to design programs, practices, and innovations that ground the values and culture of the organization. With such a scattered and diverse workforce, it may be impossible to get everyone to think of himself or herself as a "Ford man" or a "Ford woman." It is possible, however, to implement measures that forge some sort of common identity — and effectively answer the question, "Who are

The Challenges of Outsourcing

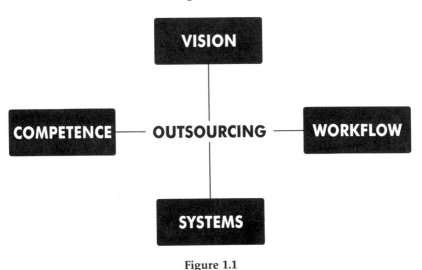

Figure 1.1

we?" Then, and only then, can you address the critical question, "Where are we going?"

Workflow. Outsourcing is, in essence, the outward manifestation of a radically different acceptance of how work can and will get done. It thus has a dramatic impact on human resources, the function that has historically been charged with establishing the traditional principles and rules of the workplace. In the past, HR could fulfill this sacred duty through the almighty job description — by simply telling people what their job entailed and what supervisor they had to answer to. This no longer suffices. Because of outsourcing, what to do and who to "report to" have become outdated answers to markedly new questions. The key is not to define jobs, but to define workflow. What work is best done inside the organization and what work should be sent out? How do you integrate the in-house and the external to create efficient service or effective product? Outsourcing challenges the HR professional to create and implement work processes that tie all of this together, bringing seamless order out of potential chaos, and to redefine the new values, principles, and rules that govern how work gets done. It is up to HR to build a workforce that knows how to work differently in this new age.

Competence. The new era of outsourcing calls for new competencies — a set of skills, knowledge, abilities, and behaviors that will drive your new strategy to organizational excellence. It is human resources that must identify these competencies and then make sure that its organization is filled with people who possess them. In one sense, this is familiar ground for HR professionals; "training and development," however that term is defined, has long been one of the profession's bailiwicks. On the other hand, identifying and cultivating competencies in this new world requires innovation and foresight that exceeds the normal assessment, measurement, and evaluation protocol. The inquiry is no longer the discrete, "What kind of skills and knowledge does a person need to perform this specific job?" Instead, the question is now, "What competencies must a person possess to achieve high performance within a scattered, diverse workforce and network-like strategic architecture?" The answer will, of course, vary depending on the particular job and the particular situation; some of the competencies that might be required to drive the outsourcing organization forward are communication skills, teamwork, relationship building, collaboration, cooperation, and the ability to exert influence without control. HR must build the organization's overall core competence and fashion the roles of employees in creating it.

Systems. Lastly, HR professionals face the challenge of devising effective systems that support the organization's work amidst and through outsourcing. The answer here does not lie with static policies and procedures but, rather, dynamic programs, practices, and innovations around traditional HR areas such as benefits, payroll, employee and labor relations, and recruiting. Consider the latter, for example. In the old days, HR leaders could proudly — and justifiably — say, "They want good people, and we find them." While this mantra is not completely dead, the rules of the game have clearly broadened and changed. The key now is to find and develop the best workers at the lowest cost. This requires a more systematic approach that incorporates programs, practices, and innovations that include but go beyond simply placing an ad or enlisting a search firm. Without such systems to support recruiting and other critical functions, the outsourcing organization will soon find itself unsupported and adrift. The challenge for HR is to establish the systems that ground the effort. In a transformed organization, systems can supply some commonalty throughout the organization.

The Opportunities of Outsourcing

In the course of meeting outsourcing's challenges, HR leaders should seize outsourcing's opportunities. If they do, they will become the internal outsourcing experts and consultants for their organizations. The payoff of such a role is considerable: the status of strategic business partner.

There is a subtle yet critical distinction at play here. Meeting outsourcing's challenges is essentially reactive in nature; even if you do not want to confront these tasks, you might have to as more and more functions in your firm turn to outsourcing. Seizing outsourcing's opportunities, on the other hand, calls for a proactive gameplan, one of action rather than reaction.

Although you need not take the steps necessary to take hold of the outsourcing movement, you should. In fact, does human resources really have a choice in becoming the central, knowledge-based outsourcing experts of the organization? The alternative is far less appealing — to wait to become outsourced yourself. Indeed, if you do not take control of the movement, it may well overtake you. But what in particular does becoming the outsourcing expert/consultant for the organization and taking the hold of the outsourcing movement actually entail? In a certain sense, this involves leadership by example — for if human resources can, through outsourcing, transform *itself* into a lower cost, higher quality service provider, other segments of the organization will naturally look to HR for outsourcing advice and counsel. But this is only a small part of the story. Besides using HR as a model for how to practice outsourcing, we recommend that human resources take several well-defined action steps that place it at the crest of the movement up, down, and across the entire organization. In particular; human resources should:

- Develop tools and methods that will allow managers to create mental models that force them to question the assumptions that are driving their theory and enable them to determine where they want to go, with or without outsourcing.[10]

- Develop databases and a benchmarking approach that can be used to measure in-house performance against external competition.[11]

- Establish a strategic approach to outsourcing that can serve as the practical model for determining which functions or services (if any) should be outsourced — any why they should be outsourced.[12]

- Establish clear and practical guidelines on how to outsource — how to select the right vendor, how to enter the right contract, and how to manage the outsourcing venture.[13]

- Establish a clear process for assessing, measuring, and evaluating outsourcing decisions.[14]

- Offer and provide consulting services to the rest of the organization around outsourcing and change management.

To take these action steps and serve as such an internal outsourcing expert/consultant, human resources must develop and use tools that elicit the confidence of managers and build the trust of the workforce. Who better to build such tools than the HR professional? That is, after all, much of what he or she does for a living. Moreover, to provide such consulting support, HR professionals must walk a thin, delicate line, balancing the roles of internal consultant on outsourcing against the needs of the organization. Under no circumstances can the HR professional sacrifice his or her objectivity by stepping out of his or her consultant role and advocating outsourcing. After all, outsourcing is an option that should not be sold; the HR professional must be prepared to present and discuss other options (in-house agencies, joint ventures, strategic alliances, partnerships, the status quo, etc.), as well.

With those caveats, the role of outsourcing consultant should hardly be a stretch for most HR professionals. The job, after all, depends greatly on facilitation and coordination — a natural role for HR professionals to play because of their skills in communication, administration, and relationship building. In fact, many HR professionals are already acting as the organizational consultant on outsourcing; a recent study estimates that HR departments play a role in about 65 percent of all company outsourcing cases, up from about 35 percent in the past.[15] To our minds, the number should be closer to 100 percent, because HR is the natural provider of consulting assistance to the line around outsourcing and the management of change that accompanies it.

And through such consulting assistance, human resources can become the strategic business partner to the line organization. Applying Chris Argyris's thinking, when it comes to whether the human resources function is a strategic business partner, there is a great dichotomy between espoused theory (the way you say things are) and theory in use (the way things actually are).[16] The espoused theory is that HR is already a strategic business partner and need not become involved in outsourcing because it already creates competitive advantage and is untouchable. The theory-in-use, however, is that HR has been a casual observer and occasional participant in the process of outsourcing and is very much vulnerable — and touchable — in its tenuous status as strategic business partner.

In the final analysis, line managers today face enormous challenges around a common theme: to do more/better for less in a world economy with obstacles at every turn. On the receiving end, "value added" for line managers means greater efficiency, effectiveness, and productivity. On the giving end, "value added" for human resources means understanding the critical business issues facing line managers and determining how much and what you can do to create more stakeholder value. In order to be a full-fledged strategic partner, HR must thus add value — real value — to the partnership.

In a peculiar way, all of the recent turbulence in business — and the fact that the importance of humans is now universally recognized but the importance of human resources is not — is really a blessing in disguise for human resources. For too long, HR has been wed to a traditional mission that is doomed in the new realities and the new business model. HR leaders who know where their bread is buttered have correctly concluded that the new mission for HR is to become the strategic business partner to line managers. And the smart HR leaders have recognized that outsourcing is a vehicle to becoming such a partner — because outsourcing essentially involves the movement of people and work outside of the organization, and because outsourcing is about dramatically impacting the lives of people, which traditionally has been a critical differentiating, value-added function of human resources.

To take charge of outsourcing, however, HR must put a stake in the ground around outsourcing as its responsibility. In the end, it's all about control. What gives HR the right and responsibility for guiding outsourcing strategy within the organization is outsourcing's cultural and people-related impacts. To fulfill this responsibility, however, HR must create an outsourcing model and process for the organization that will convince the organization that HR has the right and responsibility to serve as the strategic business partner around outsourcing — and that will establish human resources as *the* expert and *the* consultant on outsourcing within the organization.

• • • • •

A challenge. And an opportunity. To view outsourcing as anything different — a mere task or a threat, for instance — would be shortsighted and foolhardy. It would also be unfortunate, because outsourcing is a clear pathway to becoming a strategic business partner.

Endnotes

1. Michael E. Porter, *Competitive Advantage* (New York: The Free Press, 1985). For one prominent example of a work that argues that people are crucial to organizational success, *see* Dave Ulrich and Dale Lake, *Organizational Capability* (New York: John Wiley & Sons, 1990).
2. Allan M. Mohrman, Jr. and Edward E. Lawler, III, "Human Resource Management: Building A Strategic Partnership," *Organizing For The Future* (San Francisco: Jossey-Bass Publishers, 1993), pp. 229–230.
3. Mohrman and Lawler, p. 231.
4. *See, e.g.,* Stanley Nollen and Helen Axel, *Managing Contingent Workers* (New York: Amacom, 1996) (discussing the contingent workforce and employee leasing); Steven L. Goldman, Roger N. Nagel, and Kenneth Preiss, *Agile Competitors And Virtual Organizations* (New York: Van Nostrand Reinhold, 1995) (discussing virtual organizations); David Limerick and Bert Cunnington, *Managing The New Organization* (San Francisco: Jossey-Bass Publishers, 1993) (discussing network organizations); Ron Ashkenas, Dave Ulrich, Todd Jick, and Steve Kerr, *The Boundaryless Organization* (San Francisco: Jossey-Bass Publishers, 1995) (discussing boundaryless organizations); and Sally Helgesen, *The Web Of Inclusion* (New York: Currency/Doubleday, 1995) (discussing webs of inclusion).
5. *See, e.g.,* James A. Welch and P. Ranganeth Nayak, "Strategic Sourcing: A Progressive Approach To The Make-Or-Buy Decision," *Academy Of Management Executive*, 1992 Vol. 6 No. 1, p. 23.
6. Richard A. Jacobs, "The Invisible Workforce: How To Align Contract And Temporary Workers With Core Organizational Goals," *National Productivity Review*, Spring 1994, p. 170.
7. James Brian Quinn and Frederick G. Hilmer, "Strategic Outsourcing," *Sloan Management Review*, Summer 1994, pp. 43–55. *See also* James Brian Quinn, *Intelligent Enterprise* (New York: The Free Press, 1992).

8. For a list of resources that examine outsourcing in general and in specific business contexts, *see* the Bibliographic Notes for this chapter at the end of this book.
9. Goldman, Nagel, and Preiss, p. 166.
10. *See* Chapter Five herein.
11. *See* Chapter Five herein.
12. *See* Chapter Five herein.
13. *See* Chapters Seven through Nine herein.
14. *See* Chapter Ten herein.
15. Brenda Paik Sunoo and Jennifer J. Laabs, "Winning Strategies For Outsourcing Contracts," *Personnel Journal*, March 1994, p. 70.
16. Chris Argyris, Robert Putnam, and Diana McLain Smith, *Action Science* (San Francisco: Jossey-Bass Publishers, 1985), pp. 80–101.

Chapter Two

A Report From the Field

Outsourcing is hardly new to the human resources world. For some time, human resource professionals have outsourced certain HR services and functions (notably, benefits administration and payroll) to external providers. Recently, however, outsourcing has seemingly taken on greater importance. In this era of reengineering, restructuring, and organizational change, outsourcing is now viewed as a strategic option for the delivery of a wide range of HR services — and as a structural necessity for the modern day HR department.

At least this is the perception one would ascertain from the literature. But what is the reality? How pervasive is the practice of outsourcing in HR? Who in the human resource world is actually outsourcing? How much are they outsourcing? What services and functions are they outsourcing? Why are they outsourcing? And, if they are outsourcing, what problems and issues are they encountering along the way?

To get the answers to these critical questions, we conducted a national survey of human resource executives in the fall of 1995. This chapter reports the data resulting from the survey.[1] As discussed more fully below, there are many conclusions that one can draw from this data. In the final analysis, however, we believe that the data, at a minimum, reveals the following broad yet critical facts about outsourcing:

• Most HR departments are outsourcing at least one service or function;

• Practically every HR service or function is being outsourced; and

Kelly Meehan and Tom Dimieri of Linkage, Inc. contributed to the development of this chapter.

- HR leaders are outsourcing services and functions for many different reasons.

The notion that a limited class of HR leaders are outsourcing only a selected few administrative functions for a narrow list of reasons seems inappropriate. Our survey reveals that the practice of outsourcing is pervasive, its scope is considerable, and the factors driving it are diverse.

The Survey

We surveyed approximately 1,750 human resource executives who were listed in a national directory. For the most part, the people that we surveyed were managers, directors, or vice presidents of human resources. We received written responses from 121 human resource executives, constituting a response rate of approximately seven percent.

The survey respondents represented many different organizations from across the United States. There was no significant concentration of companies in any one particular area or region. As Figure 2.1 indicates, the organizations represented by the respondents came from a wide range of industries. However, companies from three industry groups (health care, manufacturing, and finance/insurance) represented nearly two thirds of the sample.

As Figure 2.2 indicates, the size of the responding organizations varied from the very small (11 percent with less than 250 employees) to the very large (6 percent with more than 25,000 employees). Nearly two thirds of our survey respondents indicated that their HR departments had 25 employees or less.

Figure 2.3 indicates the annual revenue for the last fiscal year for those organizations represented by our survey resopndents. There was considerable variance among the represented organizations in terms of annual revenue, ranging from $5 million or less (7.3 percent) to more than $1 billion (21.8 percent).

Who Is Outsourcing

In our survey, we defined outsourcing as "having an external vendor provide a service, on a recurring basis, which would normally be performed within the organization." Pursuant to this definition, we asked our survey respondents to indicate separately for 14 different HR services and functions whether the service or function was:

• performed in-house;

• outsourced to an external service provider;

• currently performed in-house, but being considered for outsourcing; or

• not a function regularly performed by the organization.

Respondents were allowed to answer with a combination of the four options set forth above and, in fact, many gave such hybrid answers with respect to particular HR services or functions.

Nearly 91 percent of respondents indicated that they were outsourcing at least one HR service or function. The con-

Primary Business or Industry of Survey Respondents

1.	Health Care	22.5%
2.	Manufacturing	20.8%
3.	Finance/Insurance	19.2%
4.	Retail/Wholesale/Distribution	7.5%
5.	Utility/Transportation	6.7%
6.	Service	5.8%
7.	Consultant	3.3%
8.	Government	2.5%
9.	Education	.8%
10.	Other	10.9%

Figure 2.1

Organizational Size of Survey Respondents

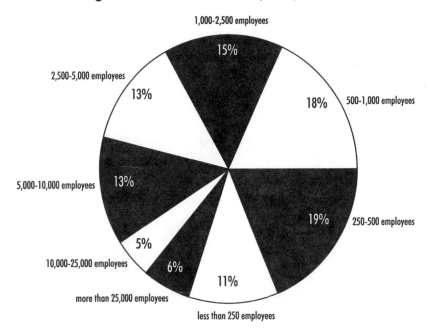

Figure 2.2

clusion that this finding suggests is obvious yet critical: *nearly everyone in HR is outsourcing something.* At the same time, few are outsourcing a lot, at least in terms of dollars. Indeed, as Figure 2.4 indicates, the vast majority of survey respondents (70 percent) indicated that the annual dollar value of HR services that they outsource is $400,000 or less, with over half of that group answering that the figure is $100,000 or less. Only 16 percent indicated the annual dollar value of HR services that they outsource is more than $1 million.

A related issue is who in the organization is making the critical outsourcing decisions. Our survey respondents indicated that decisions about what HR services to outsource, as well as which external provider to use, are most often made by the vice president of human resources. The line manager is usually involved in selecting an external provider. About 25 percent of CEOs are directly involved with the selection of the services to outsource, but only 9 percent are involved in selecting the external providers.

What They Are Outsourcing

As noted above, we asked our survey respondents to indicate which (if any) of 14 HR services or functions they were performing in-house, outsourcing, currently performing in-house but considering outsourcing, or not regularly performing at all. The answers that we received to this survey question reveal that nearly every HR service or function is being outsourced with some frequency.

Figure 2.5 demonstrates the HR services or functions that our survey respondents are outsourcing. The most frequently outsourced HR service or function is outplacement (64 percent), followed by training delivery (46 percent), training development (40 percent), relocation services (31 percent), and compensation planning (31 percent). The services and functions that are most frequently performed by both external service providers *and* by in-house employees are training delivery (34 percent), training development (31 percent), and compensation planning (20 percent).

And what HR services and functions are the least frequently outsourced? As Figure 2.5 demonstrates, our survey respondents indicated that training administration

Annual Revenue of Survey Respondents for Last Fiscal Year

Under $5 million	7.3%
$5 to $20 million	8.2%
$20 to $50 million	13.6%
$50 to $100 million	9.1%
$100 to $200 million	12.7%
$200 to $500 million	18.2%
$500 million to $1 billion	9.1%
More than $1 billion	21.8%

Figure 2.3

Annual Dollar Value of HR Services Outsourced

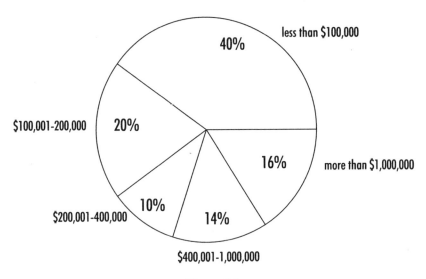

Figure 2.4

(2 percent), HR administration (3 percent), training evaluation (4 percent), HR information systems (8 percent), and health, safety, and security (12 percent) are outsourced the least. In general, respondents tend *not* to outsource administrative functions; in addition to HR and training administration, benefits administration is rarely outsourced. The flip side here concerns the HR services and functions that HR departments are keeping in-house — a list that tracks but does not match the least frequently outsourced functions. According to our survey respondents, the services and functions that are most often performed in-house are training administration (93 percent), training evaluation (86 percent), HR information systems (84 percent), recruitment, employment, and staffing (82 percent), and health, safety, and security (79 percent).

We asked our respondents if they expected the size of their HR departments to change within the next two years, and in response, 18.8 percent indicated that they expected a slight increase, 39.3 percent expected a slight decrease, 8.5 percent expected a significant decrease, and 33.3 percent expected the size to stay the same. Analyzing how an HR department's projected size over the next several years affected its various outsourcing decisions suggests some general yet valuable conclusions with respect to several HR services and functions:

- *Recruitment, Employment, and Staffing*: These functions are more likely to be performed in-house where there are no significant changes in the number of employees anticipated. The likelihood that these functions are outsourced, however, increases where the number of employees is expected to increase or decrease slightly.

HR Services/Functions That Organizations Outsource

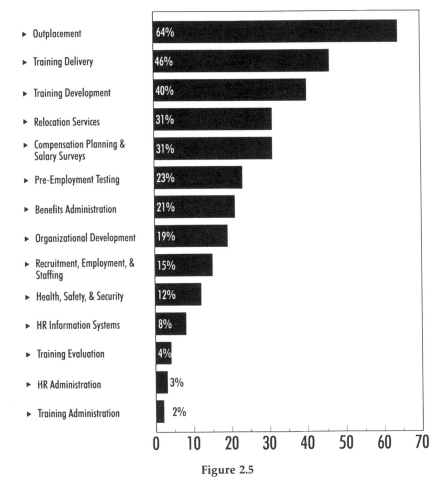

▶ Outplacement	64%
▶ Training Delivery	46%
▶ Training Development	40%
▶ Relocation Services	31%
▶ Compensation Planning & Salary Surveys	31%
▶ Pre-Employment Testing	23%
▶ Benefits Administration	21%
▶ Organizational Development	19%
▶ Recruitment, Employment, & Staffing	15%
▶ Health, Safety, & Security	12%
▶ HR Information Systems	8%
▶ Training Evaluation	4%
▶ HR Administration	3%
▶ Training Administration	2%

0   10   20   30   40   50   60   70

Figure 2.5

- *Relocation Services*: Those HR departments that are increasing in size are more likely to perform relocation in-house, whereas those that are getting smaller are more likely to outsource the function.
- *Outplacement*: The HR departments that are anticipating a significant decrease in the number of employees are most likely to outsource outplacement, while those that expect to remain stable or grow do not require the service at all.
- *HR Administration:* Outsourcing HR administration is most likely to occur in those HR departments that expect a significant decrease in the number of employees over the next two years.

Why They Are Outsourcing

We also asked our survey respondents why they are outsourcing HR services and functions. Their answers reveal no one simple reason for the phenomenon, but instead, a wide variety of rationales, depending upon the organization and the service or function being outsourced.

In general, the reason most often cited for outsourcing was to employ the expertise of specialists. A staggering **88 percent** of respondents indicated that they outsource for this reason, in whole or in part (respondents were allowed to check more than one reason). According to our data, HR departments also outsource to save time (54 percent), save money (41 percent), save administrative costs (38 percent), and focus on more strategic initiatives (30 percent). Conversely, the reasons least cited for outsourcing were because of a desire to reduce liability (7 percent), budget cuts (15 percent), and staff reductions (20 percent). Figure 2.6 demonstrates the full range of reasons for outsourcing HR services as indicated by our survey respondents.

We derive three general conclusions from this data. **First,** the fact that most respondents indicated that they outsourced to employ the expertise of specialists reveals that the desire for enhanced quality and added capabilities is perhaps *the* driving factor behind the phenomenon of

Reasons Why Organizations Outsource HR Services/Functions

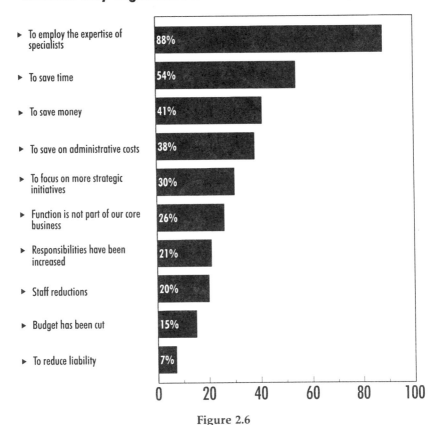

- ▸ To employ the expertise of specialists — 88%
- ▸ To save time — 54%
- ▸ To save money — 41%
- ▸ To save on administrative costs — 38%
- ▸ To focus on more strategic initiatives — 30%
- ▸ Function is not part of our core business — 26%
- ▸ Responsibilities have been increased — 21%
- ▸ Staff reductions — 20%
- ▸ Budget has been cut — 15%
- ▸ To reduce liability — 7%

Figure 2.6

outsourcing. **Second,** while saving money and focusing on strategic initiatives are, indeed, important variables in the decision to outsource, they are not quite as important as indicated in the literature. **Third,** no significant statistical relationship was found between a decrease in the size of the HR department and outsourcing. A small percentage of respondents indicated that they were outsourcing for the downsizing-related reasons of cuts in budget (15 percent) or reductions in staff (20 percent).

The survey results further suggest that certain HR services or functions are outsourced for certain reasons, as follows:

- *Training delivery* is often outsourced to save money, cope with increased responsibilities, and better manage HR staff reductions.
- *Training development* and *health/safety/security* are often outsourced to save money.
- *Recruitment, employment, and staffing* are outsourced primarily to save money, better manage the increased responsibilities of HR, and deal with budget cuts.
- *Relocation services* are often outsourced to employ the expertise of specialists.
- *Outplacement* is often outsourced to reduce liability.
- *Benefits administration* is often outsourced because of a desire to focus on more strategic initiatives, as well as to manage increased responsibilities.
- *HR administration* is often outsourced to employ the expertise of specialists, as well as a result of budget cuts.

What Problems and Issues They Are Encountering When Outsourcing

Finally, we asked our survey respondents to indicate what issues they found to be problematic when outsourcing. The issues that they cited varied considerably, suggesting that HR professionals have encountered a wide array of problems when outsourcing.

The issue that survey respondents indicated as most problematic was selecting the best contractor (22 percent), followed closely by cost (21 percent). Other problematic areas included choosing which functions to outsource (15 percent), monitoring the contractor's performance (15 percent), contractor/organization relations (14 percent), and the contractor's fit within the organization (13 percent). Further analysis suggests that, with respect to certain HR services or functions, particular issues seem to be problematic on a consistent basis when they are either outsourced entirely or performed in conjunction with an external partner. Figure 2.7 lists the prevalent problematic issues for six different HR services or functions.

Prevalent Problematic Issues for HR Services and Functions

Service/Function	Problematic Issue(s)
Training Development	• Selecting the best contractor • Cost • Monitoring contractor performance
Training Administration	• Finding the right contractor • Selecting the best contractor • Monitoring contractor performance
Training Evaluation	• Finding the right contractor • Contractor/organization relations • Contractor's fit with the organization • Selecting the best contractor
Recruitment, Employment, and Staffing	• Negotiating the contract
Benefits Administration	• Cost
HR Information Systems	• Contractor/organization relations • Finding the right contractor

Figure 2.7

In sum, our survey indicated that HR professionals are outsourcing different services and functions for different reasons, encountering different problems along the way. The survey reveals general yet valuable insights into what and why HR professionals are outsourcing. Above all, based on our survey results, it is clear that HR services and functions are being outsourced and that the trend is pervasive and increasing.

Endnotes

1. Some of these survey results were presented and analyzed in Philip J. Harkins, Stephen M. Brown, and Russell Sullivan, "Shining New Light On A Growing Trend," *HR Magazine*, December 1995, pp. 75–79. For other articles presenting survey data on outsourcing in the human resources context, and still other that discuss the overall trend of HR outsourcing (or aspects thereof), *see* the Bibliographic Notes for this chapter at the end of this book.

Chapter Three

Outsourcing and the Enterprise Value Chain

Reed A. Keller

For SunTrust Banks, a southeast regional banking institution, the decision to outsource began with organizational change and a fresh look. In 1994, the diverse, decentralized organization (the banks operated under three different names in Georgia, Florida and Tennessee) committed to faster growth and sustainable competitive advantages. The lack of centralized staff functions, senior management concluded, was costly. And a paternalistic attitude towards employees created operational inefficiencies. "We knew it was high time to start treating our employees as adults," recalled SunTrust human resources executive Lane Caruso, "letting them make their own decisions and take ownership."[1] Key to that new mindset was an understanding that some HR functions weren't adding value organizationally, and that HR needed to become a better business partner.

Outdated technology and labor intensive processes that required local HR employees to spend enormous amounts of time "handholding" the workforce explained the functions' inefficiency. The recognition that benefits administration was not — and need not become — a center of excellence for the banks soon followed. "When we started this consolidation," said Caruso, "we fully believed that nobody could do it better than we could internally." The cost of the technology — and the availability of best practice services from outside vendors — quickly changed the minds of SunTrust's leaders. By January 1995, benefits administration had been outsourced — at a savings of nearly $5 million compared to what an internal, techno-logically-updated centralized initiative would have cost. And no one, concluded Caruso, was more delighted than the HR field staffers. "They're glad to get out of the business of administration," Caruso said.[2]

SunTrust Banks — like thousands of other organizations considering outsourcing — had to first determine what HR processes it did well, and which it didn't. But the company also had to make a second judgment: whether a function was a strategic asset that was important to keep within the organization's structure. For many HR leaders, this is a step into a brave new world.

The New Perspective

In this era of hypercompetition, globalization, and fundamental shifts in the employer/employee contract, understanding that there is a new role for HR leaders and their departments to play is a requirement in the search for sustainable competitive advantage. This conclusion is documented in the Corporate Leadership Council's 1995 report, *Vision Of The Future: Role Of Human Resources In The New Corporate Headquarters*, a study that included most of the *Fortune 50*. The Council's assessment acknowledged that today's HR executive is performing in a changed business environment, one that's suffering a hangover from the business process reengineering binge of the past three years.[3] Wall Street no longer reacts favorably to cost-generated earnings improvements, such as those driven by periodic restructuring changes. The new mantra is for growth-generated earnings. In part as a consequence of the reengineering phenomenon, employees have become increasingly self-reliant.

"You will never have good customer relations until you have good employee relations," is a quote attributed to Walt Disney. It also reflects the challenge confronting most business leaders. Organizations today are pushed to establish challenging work, recognition for performance, and opportunities to advance in order to cement a productive employee-employer relationship.

These challenges and the changed business environment have shaped a new perspective on what is necessary for market success: the embrace of a knowledge-based structure to become a *knowledge enterprise*. In a knowledge enterprise, human capital emerges as the optimizing resource rather than financial, capital, or physical assets. At its essence is the value creation capability of new ideas and new knowledge. All businesses are moving in this direction; the most successful — Microsoft, Intel — already dominate their industries. In other industries (the automobile industry, for example), the 21st Century leaders will be those who are best able to leverage their human capital.

A knowledge enterprise recognizes that core competencies are the value drivers of its business, both now and, as they're enhanced, in the future. And a knowledge enterprise requires an HR organization whose cycle times match those of the line organization in developing products and services, exercising leadership, and performing operations. That role means the abandonment of HR's policy-issuing, controlling past. In this new world, traditional practices won't work. HR has to travel at the same breakneck pace as the business units with which it partners.

Today, the HR leader must prepare to help his or her organization maximize human capital and acquire the knowledge relevant to the core competencies of the business. Without this human capital development, companies lose the opportunity to substantially increase shareholder value. With its development — through an understanding of the impact of HR systems and practices on the overall enterprise, an analysis of the effectiveness of those systems and practices, and the implementation of what I call high performance work practices, where the status quo needs to be changed and improved — HR managers will shift from playing their historical role as *denominator* managers to become proactive *numerator* managers within the return on investment equation. When they do, they will emerge as business partners solutions to real business problems. At that point, HR will create value and have genuine strategic impact.

The Development of the Enterprise Value Chain

What does a knowledge enterprise look like? How does it function?

Developing human capital, to be done effectively, requires a systems perspective towards an organization. Such a perspective recognizes that organizations are dynamic and comprised of interdependent subsystems, each of which interacts with the other in complex, non-linear ways. In the knowledge enterprise model, four sub-systems — Leadership, Operations, Market, and Human Resources — are linked through three value drivers — customer preference, shareholder value, and core competencies. This linkage forms the *Enterprise Value Chain. See* Figure 3.1. In this model, core competencies are the most important of the three value drivers. Without excellence here, a business will neither maximize shareholder value, nor develop the depth of customer intimacy necessary to build long-term, profitable relationships.

Within each organizational subsystem, three core processes define the value of that system to the whole. For Leadership, the processes are to reset direction and create new vision and values; to establish investment priorities and metrics; and to create an exciting environment with a passion for winning. The core processes aligned with the Operations subsystem are to position the best people against the best opportunities; to set operating priorities and create a trend of success and improvement; and to generate superior economic returns both now and in the future. In the Market subsystem — which may be focused on either product development or customer service, depending upon the industry — the core processes are to create new knowledge and new, or improved, products or services; to provide superior value to the customer; and to establish customer loyalty and market reputation. And within the Human Resources subsystem, what's critical is to match resources to needs, hire the best, and prune non-performance; to establish a performance culture and a risk/reward framework that reflects that culture; and to develop individual and team capabilities. Each subsystem's components interact dynamically. Their "fit" or congruence — as

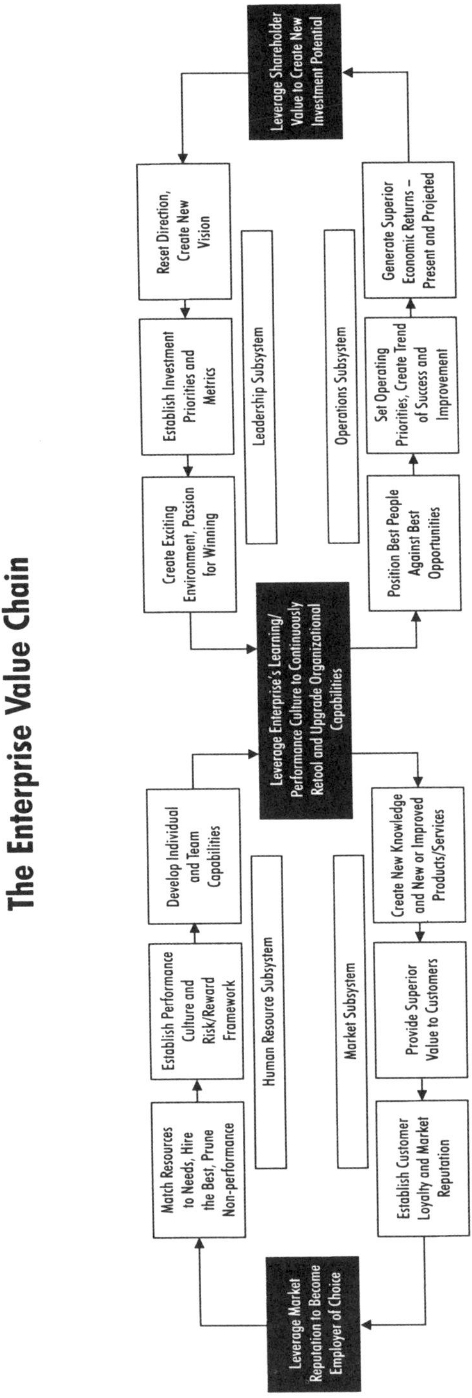

The Enterprise Value Chain

Figure 3.1

much as the appropriateness and effectiveness of each system — determines the level of overall performance.

Human Capital Development

The interconnections of the Enterprise Value Chain force HR leaders to think of their processes within the entirety of the system, rather than of HR as an isolated department. HR departments have been separated from the needs of the business overall and consumed by administrative tasks that don't have the capacity for adding value. Within the Enterprise Value Chain, the HR leader assumes a fundamentally different role: he or she must be responsible for continually advancing the organizational capabilities of the business.

In a knowledge enterprise, the HR practices that develop human capital are continuous and linked to the needs of the external environment. Hiring the best employees, developing individual and team capabilities, and retention of top performers all contribute to new organizational opportunity. And that linkage ties directly to the processes of product development and building customer relationships. Success in the external environment hinges upon the ability, skill, and motivation of an organization's people. And, conversely, the ability to attract and retain top talent depends on and is reinforced by the organization's success in the external arena.

For the HR executive, assuming this responsibility means adopting both a new perspective and a role that encompasses the entire Value Chain: the "CFO for Human Capital." It's the consequence of the realization that traditional strategic levers (such as economies of scale and proprietary technology), while still of value, cannot sustain competitive advantage and above-average profitability as they have in the past. Behavioral strategies that focus on how a firm does business in addition to where it does business are critical success factors. As CFO for Human Capital, the HR leader builds a powerful synergy by integrating people, processes, and technology into a capability or set of competencies difficult for competitors to imitate. As CFO for Human Capital, he or she also develops processes to ensure clarity of role and purpose and work systems that are linked to business goals and objectives. And, as this new type of leader, he or she ensures an organization has the right skills and competencies in place to respond to changes in the environment, marketplace, and competition. The end result is to have the right people in the right place at the right time.

The paradigm of the Enterprise Value Chain demands that HR leaders communicate differently, too. They must speak the language of *value*. By that, I mean market value added, which *Fortune* defines as the difference between total market value (the current value of a company's stock and debt) and invested capital (all the capital assembled from equity and debt offerings, bank loans, and retained earnings, with some adjustments for R&D spending).[4] In other words, it's the difference between the amount of money investors can take out and what they have put in. For the best — Coca-Cola, General Motors, Wal-Mart, Merck — market value added can total upwards of $30 billion. In the future, the HR executive will have to be able to make assertions about human capital strategies that demonstrate their incremental impact on market value added. He or she will have to show whether HR practices are building or detracting from customer loyalty. And he or she will have to have, at his or her fingertips, a balance sheet for human capital.

The Enterprise Value Chain is the foundation for that new level of communication.

Measuring the Saliency of HR's Processes

If employees are not the customers of human resources, then it follows that HR data and administrative processes are *not* proximate to the Enterprise Value Chain. Those processes, in other words, cannot be strategic. Consequently, they are the most likely candidates for outsourcing, because — for someone, ADP for payrolls, or Fidelity for investments — they *are* core processes, around which a company's identity has been built.

Let's think about the notion of processes and their relevance. Nike, the company that pits basketball star Charles

Barkley versus Godzilla and Michael Jordan against the world, doesn't actually make the sneakers its endorsers wear. Putting leather and rubber together is an activity delegated to vendors far from the company's Oregon headquarters.[5] Similarly, Pepsi-Cola lets others manufacture its bottles, and Ford Motor Company devotes no assembly line to tire manufacturing. On their value chains, these companies simply do not see much actual value in the above processes. On their Enterprise Value Chains, those business processes aren't close to the main rings of the chain.

But is mapping the saliency of HR processes on the Value Chain enough? No. Typically, today's methodologies used by management and consultants to map these processes do not help an HR organization *measure the effectiveness* of HR practices before, during, or after a process change. Where measurement does occur, it is usually qualitative and entails benchmarking against best practices and/or periodically comparing internal feedback. Some organizations go further by distilling this information into an effectiveness rating or index that may provide a slightly more quantitative measure of progress over time. And those who do quantify HR practices in hard numbers typically do so with cost-based measurements that cannot be readily applied to HR's less tangible aspects. A more compelling measure of HR effectiveness is needed — one that goes beyond capturing costs to also measuring how HR practices add value to *the bottom line.*

In addition, few, if any, of today's approaches maximize business relevance by *involving external customers* in the development of HR strategy and practices. While many HR organizations obtain input and feedback on the needs and expectations of their employees, and many involve line management in the development and execution of HR strategy and practices, they rarely involve their external customers in their HR processes and, thus, are missing a significant perspective on their realignment efforts.

Instead, you should couple mapping with two additional elements to build the strongest foundation for an outsourcing decision. **First,** you should conduct an econometric analysis of each process, using a methodology that measures, explains, and predicts the impact of those processes and investments on the economic performance and value-creating potential of the enterprise. An econometric study may use non-experimental longitudinal research and statistical analyses to estimate significant correlation between a company's system of high performance work practices and bottom-line financial performance measures. Dr. Mark A. Huselid of Rutgers University's School of Management and Labor Relations and Dr. Brian E. Becker of the State University of New York at Buffalo's School of Management are two cutting edge leaders in this field. Their work practice measures span the spectrum of HR management practices to include work design and organization, recruitment and selection, training and development, performance management, compensation, and communications. For example, their studies in 1992 revealed that a one standard deviation increase in the use of high performance work practices was associated with per-employee changes of $18,641 in higher market value and $3,814 in higher profits.[6] Continual refinement of their research and expansion of their database (approximately 1,000 companies) have produced even more persuasive results.

Second, you should hold a facilitated meeting (what I call social "laboratories") where HR executives, customers, and/or suppliers gather together to examine, define, and prioritize common values that — when aligned and leveraged — can yield joint problem-solving processes, superior service, and lasting relationships. "Tomorrow's winners will be those companies that discover how to anticipate and truly meet a customer's needs in a unique way," says author and educator David Ulrich. "In terms of specific HR strategy, tomorrow's winners will be those companies who are first to leverage a number of organizational capabilities, such as institutionalizing learning to make their intellectual capital (*i.e.*, knowledge) more productive; creating flexibility and the capacity for managing change; and effectively teaming across both internal and external organizational boundaries."[7]

With the information gathered through econometric studies and the social laboratory, HR leaders will be fully prepared to weigh outsourcing as a tool, allowing them to maintain a strong, unwavering attention to those HR processes that are core and strategic. And many will conclude that outsourcing's greatest value lies in third-party vendors' ability to create, for a business, a self-service platform that may give employees instant access to the information and decision models that affect their success and satisfaction, at work and at home.

Making the Outsourcing Decision

Last winter, the *Wall Street Journal* reported that more than 40 percent of the *Fortune 500* had recently outsourced at least one department or service, indicating that its value as such a tool is already being embraced.[8] As Richard C. Marcus, former chief executive officer of Neiman Marcus, has noted, "Most companies put undue emphasis on owning, managing and controlling every activity. There's just not enough time in the day to manage everything anymore."

What, then, are the fundamental considerations an HR leader should weigh when deciding to outsource a process when acting as CFO for Human Capital? **First,** outsourcing should give you access to best practices through your outsourcing provider. After all, your service provider has the luxury of focusing on one particular service or function. By definition, the service provider is touching a lot of companies that need the same things done — and is presumedly designing superior methods and processes to meet these needs. Whether it is cleaning offices, cutting paychecks, or running computer centers, it looks the same across corporations. That is why the outsourcer can make a business, and create both expertise and economies of scale. Best practices should include ongoing innovation in those areas where you're not going to be the innovator yourself.

Second, expect some economies of scale, greater performance improvement on balance, and, certainly, more performance stability. Outsourced services are a bit like utilities — if a company does it on its own, there is no activity that is steady throughout the year. Instead, there are peaks and valleys. And the tough thing for most staff functions is how to respond to the peaks and valleys. The temptation is to staff for the peaks and leave yourself overstaffed for the remainder of the year. That is why most companies don't generate their own power — they cannot afford to invest the capital in the generating equipment they'd need to meet their peak demands. An outsourcer should bring stability. And when you have a peak demand, they can meet it readily.

Third, change should be facilitated. Assume your outsourcing provider is delivering an effective and efficient service, at a reasonable level of innovation, with best practices. Over time, when you need to make a change (whether imposed by competition, management decisions, or government regulation) in a well-managed partnership between you and your provider, your outsourcing vendor ought to be able to help you move more quickly than you could on your own. Making decisions quickly and acting on them has become more important in business. That is the central, enduring advantage of outsourcing.

These lessons don't come easily. Consider the example of one recent company, which approached reengineering HR with the intent of taking 20 percent of their people out of the department. Our analysis suggested, however, that their recruitment — and this was a company that depended upon the quality of its workforce to compete — fell far below the industry median in performance. If the corporation simply downsized, and did it well, the savings were potentially a few million dollars — assuming the organization had 20 percent excess people. But recognizing the process' importance within the Enterprise Value Chain, and investing the resources necessary to make it among the industry's best, could make the process become an invisible asset. Recruitment's eventual effort would be to upgrade the company's operational capabilities. And that, in turn, could have a market value added impact exponentially more valuable than any downsizing.

Several million is certainly worth bending over in the middle of the road to pick up, but why not go for the billions? That is the potential value of the Human Resources subsystem as seen through the Enterprise Value Chain.

Endnotes

1. Lane Caruso and Lee Mulert, "Outsourcing — The Decision," *hr advisory*, Winter 1996, pp. 2–4.
2. *Id.*
3. Corporate Leadership Council, *Vision Of The Future: Role Of Human Resources In The New Corporate Headquarters* (New York: Corporate Leadership Council, 1995).
4. Betsy Morris, "The Wealth Builders," *Fortune*, December 11, 1995, p. 80.
5. For a more in-depth analysis of Nike's manufacturing practices and strategic outsourcing, *see* James Brian Quinn, *Intelligent Enterprise* (New York: The Free Press, 1992), pp. 60–64.
6. Mark A. Huselid and Brian E. Becker, "The Strategic Impact Of Human Resources: Building High Performance Work Systems," *hr advisory*, Summer 1995, pp. 2–6.
7. Reed Keller and William Thomas, "Breaking Through The Contemporary View Of HR Redesign," *hr advisory*, Winter 1996, p. 21.
8. Hal Lancaster, "Saving Your Career When Your Position Has Been Outsourced," *Wall Street Journal*, December 12, 1995, p. B1.

Chapter Four

Market Dynamics and the Future of HR Outsourcing

Gary L. Breitbart

The HR outsourcing industry has evolved considerably over the past decade, but it still has a long way to go to meet the demands of a rapidly changing client marketplace. As we approach the end of the century, the HR outsourcing industry is ripe for change, as economics, managerial challenges, and client needs and demands all intersect.

HR outsourcing has evolved from primarily a transaction-oriented benefits administration business to a broad industry attempting to span the strategic, planning, and transaction functions of HR. The initial vendors entered the business to supplement their other businesses — plan consulting and actuarial work, mutual fund management, payroll processing, or insurance. Providers saw the potential to enter into new partnerships with clients that represented significant new revenue opportunities.

In today's outsourcing market, everything is different. For the competitive reasons discussed below, clients today are re-examining their outsourcing objectives, demanding more than just transaction processing and administration, and pushing to expand outsourcing into the strategic functions of HR management. The vendor community therefore finds itself with yet another growth opportunity. Many current service providers are, however, ill-equipped to provide such broad services to their clients; they may lack certain necessary skills or may be limited in the capital improvements that they can make in systems and resources due to low returns on their initial investments.

Because the provider market is restricted from a functional competency and economic standpoint, it is questionable who will be able to expand their operations rapidly and efficiently enough to be successful players. Only a certain number of providers will be able to respond.

In looking at this provider dilemma primarily through the lens of one HR function — benefits administration — this chapter is intended to help HR executives gain a new understanding of the outsourcing market so that they can make better purchasing decisions and avoid errors that may be difficult and costly to correct. Recognizing that client needs will continue to drive the industry's evolution, this chapter also focuses on economics and competitive dynamics and makes some projections about how those needs will likely be met.

Outsourcing Today

Competitive Factors Driving Outsourcing

In a recent *Wall Street Journal* article, management guru Peter Drucker predicted that in 10 to 15 years organizations would be outsourcing all functions that are support rather than revenue-producing.[1] The implication is that firms that fail to do so will be operating at a disadvantage vis-a-vis their competitors, who by outsourcing non-core functions will lower their overall operating costs and improve their service delivery.

Drucker was right on the mark in highlighting the dilemma facing HR executives. Caught amidst downsizings, cost-cutting, and the increasing management, employee, and regulatory demands for higher levels of information and reporting, these executives must focus on transforming their departments from paper-intensive transaction processing *cost centers* to strategic, value-added HR and benefits management *profit centers*. If Drucker is right and companies will indeed consider only core business processes for investment and purchase all non-core functions (*i.e.*, outsource), then HR and benefits administration are the next logical targets in corporate re-engineering efforts that have already worked their way through manufacturing, operations, sales, and marketing.

Therefore, the primary factors driving the trend towards HR outsourcing are those having a direct impact on a company's overall competitive marketplace position:

- corporate re-engineering to focus on core business functions;
- reorientation of the HR function away from transaction processing toward strategic planning;
- increased employee and management demands for service, including transactions, information, and reporting;
- increased regulatory and compliance requirements; and
- cost control pressures.

Meeting Outsourcing Objectives

Firms that moved to outsourcing early in the game did so theoretically on the assumption that providers would generate savings by achieving scale in operations and spreading these savings over a wide range of clients; be more successful with continuing investments in new technology; and do a better analytical job as a result of managing data and processes, thus allowing the client to achieve greater efficiency and quality in the HR and benefits program design.

In reality, however, the primary motivation on the client side was financial, *i.e.*, the desire to lower transaction processing costs and deal with increasing workload and less staff. Providers responded with outsourcing models designed to accommodate administrative processes, achieve scale, and drive down costs. Providers have had a difficult time executing these models, however. Even if the models achieved efficient scale operation, the expanded investment that many required has resulted in low profit margins for providers.

The challenge now for providers is to return to the clients' original, theoretical buying premises and deliver the strategic side of the equation, thereby adding value and lifting operating performance. To meet this challenge, providers must not only make further investment at a time when they can least afford it — and within the context of a capital-starved industry — but must also develop a different, more comprehensive set of competencies. The important point is this: clients (especially those who have been disappointed in any way with the results obtained from existing providers) will not hesitate to move their business to providers who can respond the most efficiently to the original theoretical buying premise and who have a plan to effectively deliver higher value strategic services.

Current Outsourcing Models

Firms of all sizes in diverse industries are currently using HR outsourcing in one form or another. Although there is consensus as to the basic definition of outsourcing (*i.e.*, the transfer of the management or administration of a process or function from in-house staff to an outside service provider), actual outsourcing models have evolved over time and have been determined by such factors as industry type, size of company (number of employees), corporate culture and management strategy, in-house technological capabilities, and company financial structure. Outsourcing models run the gamut from total outsourcing to hybrid arrangements attempting to create the best of both insourcing and outsourcing. The following are the common approaches in the market today:

- **total outsourcing:** all aspects of planning and transactional services are outsourced to a single provider
- **functional:** only specific functions, generally of an administrative nature or which require significant investment to realize returns from scale, are transferred to one or more outside service providers
- **integrated (what we call Worksharing[sm])[2]:** many or all functions are outsourced to a fully interlinked network of providers (which may include some in-house groups)[3]

Keep in mind, however, that HR is a dynamic, needs-driven function that requires increasing flexibility. Because the outsourcing models that predominate today rely on highly standardized service delivery, they are fast becoming obsolete as rapid industry changes occur in demand, the technological environment, and economics of the industry. For example, early total outsourcing models were based on creating customized programs for a few very large anchor clients. Although vendors hoped to standardize their processes and systems from these customized offerings, they unfortunately did not lend themselves well to standardization. Vendors who attempted this reverse engineering endeavor have had significant systems programming and operating problems and are ill-prepared for the imminent market share battle discussed below.

Who Is Providing What

Because outsourcing is still a relatively new and evolving "product," firms in different but related industries have jumped in to meet the demand over the past several years. Their reasons were, with a few exceptions, defensive rather than offensive, *i.e.*, to protect an existing client relationship and the profit stream that the relationship represented. The more forward-thinking firms viewed outsourcing as a way to expand their business repertoire and created internal divisions, subsidiaries, or spin-offs to manage and market the new "product line" accordingly. As a result, today we see a wide range of firms in the outsourcing business, including insurance companies, TPAs and payroll providers, mutual fund/investment firms, management consultants, technological consultants and systems integrators, and even coalitions of large-scale users.

There has been a somewhat logical economic progression regarding which functions are outsourced, from low-value activities such as information/transaction processing and recordkeeping, to higher-value processes such as case management, plan design, recruiting and training, and vendor management. This progression essentially mirrors the shift in corporate strategy from mere cost cutting to more strategic planning and value (profit). The majority of existing outsourcing arrangements, however, continue to include mostly lower-value functions such as benefits administration and employee service for core plans (*i.e.*, medical, life, and disability spending accounts), actuarial based recordkeeping for defined contribution (DC) and defined benefit (DB) plans, and high-transaction services (*i.e.*, payroll, benefits enrollments, and employee service center support).[4]

Outsourcing Tomorrow

Where We're Headed

While it's true that many organizations originally turned to outsourcing to cut costs rapidly and eliminate operationally intense HR administration functions, they were also looking for long-term economic advantages. Many weren't able to invest in new technology or develop expert systems or processes that would allow them to lower costs and implement fundamental program design changes. (This was especially true, for example, in gathering and using healthcare data to impact quality of care and cost containment issues as opposed to negotiating premium reductions as firms had typically done in the past.) Over the next several years, as initial cost savings provided by outsourcing are passed on to clients, vendors will face increasing pressure from clients to improve systems and processes, as well as to expand services to provide high-level expertise and consultative advice in areas not traditionally outsourced, such as:

- workers compensation integration;
- high-level utilization review and quality of care measurements for health care;
- integration of competency models into workforce evaluation; and
- business process re-engineering and design.

Providers will be challenged to respond to expanded client needs by altering their services, capabilities, and cultures. For example, the administrative outsourcing which

many providers have focused on is a difficult business —
and one that's highly competitive and filled with seasonal
demand, low operating margins, complex operating rules,
large and continuing systems investment requirements,
and high personnel requirements. Many providers who
built the infrastructure to compete in this arena may find
that they constructed the wrong kind of delivery architecture, ill-suited to support more conceptually based processes and services. Success in administrative outsourcing
will also depend on a specific set of skills and competencies which are indispensable to the delivery of high-vol-
ume, high-quality employee service that can also meet
other transactional related client expectations. In particular, as we move forward, clients will look to their outsourcing providers to possess the following capabilities:

- financial and technical means to sustain continuous
  systems development;
- ability to manage systems throughout a life cycle;
- discipline to process, including standardization of
  workflows and documentation;
- consistent customer service orientation;
- application and process engineering skills;
- understanding of benefits plan design and application
  expertise;
- teleservicing experience;
- ability to achieve scale in operations; and
- ability to adapt to changing client needs.

As acquiring these capabilities is combined with expand-
ing client demand for newer and better technology, providers may face prolonged periods of low or negative profit
margins and the need for significant increases in capital
investment.

The Coming Shakeout

The impact of all the above has been a supply side that is
severely constrained, with demand for services far exceed-
ing the ability of providers to supply them. Given the

increasing client demand pressure, the survivors will be the providers that can find a way to reach scale, garner sufficient market share to drive profitability, and secure the incremental investment to build new capabilities and competencies. These providers will meet demand most efficiently and build their outsourcing practices into profitable, stand-alone ventures. Those who can't reach scale or attract the needed investment (versus other internal operations in their parent organizations) will be forced to retrench and transition their businesses to protect their reputations with clients. Below we forecast how we see the outsourcing market evolving over both the short term (0–3 years) and the medium term (3–6 years).

Short term (0–3 years): We see a shift in the supply and demand characteristics of the HR outsourcing industry. Most benefit administration vendors will be completing the infrastructure of their systems in 1996 and the first half of 1997. With this development, available capacity will expand tremendously. During this period, we can expect to see providers cut pricing to attract volume and drive scale, allowing them to capture market share. Although investment in systems capacity to date has been significant (we estimate total industry system investment in benefits administration call centers alone of more than $150 million), only a few firms have gone past break-even into true profitability in service delivery. They are either still in the process of building their systems and are unable to handle enough volume to reach scale, or they are still building processes.

As a result, it is highly probable that a price war will develop by early 1997 as providers try to increase market share and support enough employee lives in their centers to reach optimal operating scale. They will most likely do this by targeting middle-market companies (5,000–20,000 employees) as clients. Our research indicates that an estimated 30 percent drop in both setup and transactions fees can be expected over the next 18 months.

At the same time, overall industry revenues must grow rapidly ($150–200 million over the next three years) to help the industry reach operating break-even. Yet we estimate that providers may need an additional $60–80 million of investment to complete systems and processes that are already under way and to expand service competencies. This means that the financial challenge facing providers is extreme and may only worsen with time.

Medium term (3–6 years): We believe that there will be an industry consolidation, with more efficient providers emerging. This provider configuration may include some new entrants, primarily systems and related providers eager to gain fast, low-cost access to a growing revenue source. For the most part, consolidations will occur, with older players combining resources and competencies through mergers/acquisitions (to gain scale or market share, technological advantage, or financial relief) or partnerships/ strategic alliances (to improve competitive position through access to new technologies or functional expertise).

The outsourcing areas of most benefit consulting firms will face a capital shortage and their operating margins in outsourcing will continue to be considerably lower than those derived from their standard array of services. These firms will be looking for partners who have stronger cash flow and capital reserves. Two such potential partners are as follows:

- Insurance companies, who will have the capital strength but who have historically not done well at managing technology throughout the life cycle, will become potential partners. These firms will likely need to supplant a narrow service line focused on health care to compete effectively or will need help technologically. Expansion of the administrative side of these businesses will then fall primarily to their partners.

- Technology providers and systems integrators without functional HR and benefits expertise will not be able to provide stand-alone value and will likely become the partner of choice for benefits firms and insurers.

The concept of partnering for strategic reasons is not new — the early alliances forged by AT&T Transtech/ Watson–Wyatt Worldwide and by PeopleSoft/ADP (which also bought Williams Thatcher Rand, a benefits consultancy) are familiar to those in the industry. Execution has not always been smooth, however, due to differences in corporate strategy or operating styles. Having learned from early mistakes, today's players are attempting new models that may have greater potential for success. For example, benefits consultant William Mercer, systems integrator ISSC, and payroll processor Paychex have been known to bid together and are looking for synergy by combining their respective benefits, systems, and payroll expertise to meet new client interests. On the other hand, Watson-Wyatt Worldwide and State Street Bank have recently joined forces to seek increased market share by using a single-provider model ("one stop shopping") marketed as "integrated" consulting. This case is a prime example of two firms leveraging existing systems infrastructure of one (Watson-Wyatt Worldwide) with the high defined contribution transaction plan volume of the other (State Street Bank) to spread costs and reach scale more quickly.

However strong the functional competencies of the partners may be, the most important component of the long-term staying power on the provider side is capital for continuing investment. Those who have it, or the means to acquire it, will survive — and those who don't will fall by the wayside.

If providers are to keep pace with rapidly escalating demand, investment must be directed at three areas. **First,** providers will have to invest continuously in new technology and retool systems to provide additional scale and drive unit costs down for transaction processing and recordkeeping. **Second,** they must invest to achieve a higher level of functionality that allows them to achieve true HR management, which would include, at a minimum, process engineering/design and documentation, HR staffing and recruiting, vendor management, and benefits plan design, as well as the following new formats:

- better care delivery and more intelligent automation;
- integration of workers compensation and disability case management;
- increased use of utilization review processes and clinical effectiveness modeling to leverage data made available by improved systems and databases; and

- integration of payroll, benefits, HRIS, and HR administration.

Third, they must invest to cover the cost of providing new analytic and strategic management capabilities.

After the Shakeout

Some providers will not be able to restructure their business to meet client demand, due to either capital deficiency or fear of entering into entangling alliances with other providers. Others may be willing and able to restructure their business, but may not be able to do it fast enough or efficiently to reach the scale required to meet client demand.

What if providers are unable to respond fast enough? The most likely scenario is that some early outsourcing clients (typically the very largest corporations) will pull back from their early commitments to outsourcing and pursue one of two avenues: (1) shifting the administrative burden to another outsourcing partner with greater financial stability (*i.e.,* the insurance provider), or (2) revisiting the insourcing option. In the first case, the insurance providers will have to assume administration from other stand-alone providers or pay for the outsourcing themselves through some form of operating alliance.

The very large *Fortune 1000* firms (25,000+ employees) are more likely to return to insourcing for their future needs because of availability of capital, internal resources, and sufficient volume. The availability of newer, more efficient, and more economical client/server (enterprise) computing capabilities will provide large companies with the means for cost-effective insourcing, while continuing cost pressures will virtually guarantee a push for radical benefits simplification and employee self-service (again supported by new technology). We estimate that up to 70 percent of *Fortune 1000* firms will convert to a client/server-supported insourcing model by the year 2001.

The loss of a portion of the large client segment will put continuing financial pressure on providers who may respond by merging or forming strategic alliances and partnerships. As mentioned previously, one result will be fierce competition in the middle market as providers attempt to increase market share by targeting that segment for new business.

Even though some large firms may opt for an insourcing solution, however, the market for total outsourcing is still likely to grow in this segment. Because of advances in systems and processes, we estimate that implementation time for a total outsourcing relationship will shrink from the current 24-36 months to less than 18 months. We further estimate that conversions to a total outsourcing model will expand that market to the range of $500 million per annum by the year 1999. Despite the increase in total outsourcing, this model will most likely achieve no more than a 50 percent market penetration in this segment, primarily because demand currently exceeds both realizable and hardware capacity (keeping price levels high in the near term). Finally, the market penetration of outsourcing for individual functions will vary considerably by client size, with defined contribution the most frequently outsourced benefits function by far, at around 88 percent of firms using outsourcing.

For the remaining client market, *i.e.*, non-insourcing *Fortune 1000* firms and middle market firms, the **outsourcing model of choice will most likely be some form of totally integrated outsourcing**. The conversion to totally integrated outsourcing will be expedited by the arrival of state-of-the-art systems infrastructure, interface standardization, and other yet to be developed system tools. These third generation client/server-based outsourcing centers will feature:

- computer system interconnectivity between and among client and providers;
- enhanced employee access to information using IVR technology, kiosks, the Internet, and PC-based WANs and LANs; and
- cutting-edge, screen-based functions such as case management, hypertext, and imaging.

Because the integrated outsourcing solution eliminates financial and technical subsidization of services (which occurs in a "one stop" outsourcing situation), encourages better economic choices by functional providers, and reduces the considerable risks associated with single-provider arrangements, it will further inhibit the growth of total outsourcing in this segment.

Finally, an important consequence of expanded integrated outsourcing solutions and the need for high-value services will be the creation of a parallel niche in the provider market that will be filled by highly specialized general outsourcing consultants. These "big picture" consultants will have broad industry knowledge and experience. They will provide value to their clients by delivering strategic and analytic services such as systems architecture and benefits plan design, and more. Their most important role, however, will be assisting clients in developing workable, long-term outsourcing strategies, including risk assessment and management and vendor evaluation, selection, and management.

Endnotes

1. Peter F. Drucker, "The Network Society," *Wall Street Journal*, March 29, 1995, p. A12.
2. Worksharing[sm] is a service mark of Alexander & Alexander Consulting Group.
3. For some other specific approaches to outsourcing or alternative approaches to outsourcing, *see* Chapters Five and Six herein.
4. *See* Chapter Two herein for some data on the HR services or functions currently being outsourced and an analysis of that data.

PART TWO

MODELS

Understanding outsourcing is one thing; actually doing it is another. How do you decide whether you should outsource one of your services or functions? Moreover, how do you pinpoint the particular services or functions — if any — that are appropriate for outsourcing? Equally important, how can you identify the reasons that you should outsource? And are there other approaches besides outsourcing that you can employ to meet your objectives?

In this part of the book, we present two models that you can access and use in answering these critical questions. In Chapter Five, we set forth a strategic approach to outsourcing. Our broad, contextual approach focuses on a functional model designed to reveal not only what you should outsource but also why you should outsource — your all-important strategic objectives. Then, in Chapter Six, Merrill Anderson of NCR Worldwide Services sets forth an alternative approach to outsourcing — the shared services model that he and others designed and implemented at Amoco Corporation. While there are certainly other approaches that you could employ here, the two models set forth in this part of the book are designed to provide you with the answers to the critical threshold questions that you face when considering outsourcing or some other strategic partnership.

Chapter Five

A Strategic Approach to Outsourcing

To date, the literature related to outsourcing has concentrated on implementation, the "how tos" of outsourcing. Although implementation raises a host of crucial issues that deserve attention (*see* Chapters Seven through Ten for a thorough examination of these issues), there is a critical threshold question before you reach the implementation stage — namely, what should you outsource? In this chapter, we outline a systematic, strategic approach to outsourcing that the human resource professional can access and use when deciding which service or function should be outsourced, within HR or the organization at large.

This seemingly narrow inquiry has far broader implications. While outsourcing has been an acceptable business practice for some time now, the phenomenon of widespread, multi-functional use of the practice is very recent. Outsourcing in the 1990s has become a component of building the strategic architecture of the organization so that it can remain competitive in today's changing, unpredictable business world. Taking a strategic approach to outsourcing not only can produce the business results that you desire in the short-term, but can also help create a transformed organization that can compete in the new economy on a long-term basis.

And competing in this new economy is not easy. The marketplace is fluid, the economy turbulent, and competition worldwide and fierce. The best organizations have responded to these challenges by developing a short-term strategy of survival and a long-term strategy designed to transform themselves into companies that can adapt to (and in fact reflect) the new world order. These organizations recognize that knowledge has become the new capital and know-how the pathway to competitive advantage; they compete on the basis of price-for-performance and best-in-class; and they succeed in this unpredictable environment by establishing market dominance in an identified, focused business.

And outsourcing has become a critical part of the strategic architecture for most, if not all, of these successful organizations. These companies do not view outsourcing as a trend or a threat but, rather, as a tool that can help them compete in the new world order. They see outsourcing as a vehicle to focus on their core competence, acquire the core competencies of other companies, and sculpt an organizational structure that is lean, flexible, and decentralized. When done properly and appropriately, outsourcing can indeed provide the organization with:

- a more flexible structure, reducing overhead and costs;
- access to expertise, technology, and additional capability;
- resources that enable you to focus on your core competence (and not waste time on less important functions); and
- the opportunity to strike strategic alliances with best-in-class companies that, in turn, help you solidify your own status as best-in-class.

This is not to say that outsourcing is a panacea. It isn't. In some instances, outsourcing clearly will not be the answer to a specific problem; in others, outsourcing the right things in the right way for the right reasons will not only be the discrete solution to a discrete problem but will also be a springboard to competitive advantage. Looking at it through a different prism, outsourcing can properly represent either a small part or a major building block of your strategic architecture. Outsourcing is an option — and, like other options, it should be exercised only when appropriate.

How, then, does the human resources professional know when to exercise the option of outsourcing? The model that we set forth below is designed to reveal a practical, strategic answer to that question in a wide array of circumstances. Equally important, however, is the mindset that the HR professional adopts toward outsourcing when using this model. You could, for instance, take a "wait and see" approach to outsourcing, waiting until the "trend" crests or continues before deciding whether to formulate a game plan on outsourcing. Alternatively, you could assume a defensive posture toward outsourcing — build a fortress, circle the wagons. Departmental pride or organizational politics may suggest such approach, but the realities of the new world order make it a prescription for professional suicide.

Instead, we recommend that you take a proactive, systematic approach to outsourcing — one that recognizes what outsourcing can potentially do for your own HR department and HR's status within the organization at large (*see* Chapter One for a fuller discussion of the opportunities presented by outsourcing). The centerpiece of such an approach is to develop an analytical framework as to what should stay and what should go. The model discussed below provides such a framework.

The Outsourcing Model

Figure 5.1 sets forth an outsourcing model that HR professionals can access and use when deciding which services or function — if any — to outsource. The model has potential application with respect to HR services and functions (where the HR professional is considering outsouring to improve the efficiency and effectiveness of his or her own department), as well as non-HR services and functions (where the HR professional is advising the line organization in a consultant capacity). Either way, the model does not regard outsourcing as a quick fix to reduce payroll, cost, or overhead, but, instead, treats outsourcing as a strategic decision that can help build the type of department/organization that will succeed in today's environment.

While it may be tempting to make a snap decision on the basis of how well you perform the function or whether you currently have the capacity to perform the function, such a narrow inquiry usually does not yield successful outsourcing results. Remember, the best organizations have market dominance, superior product or service, and the

The Outsourcing Model

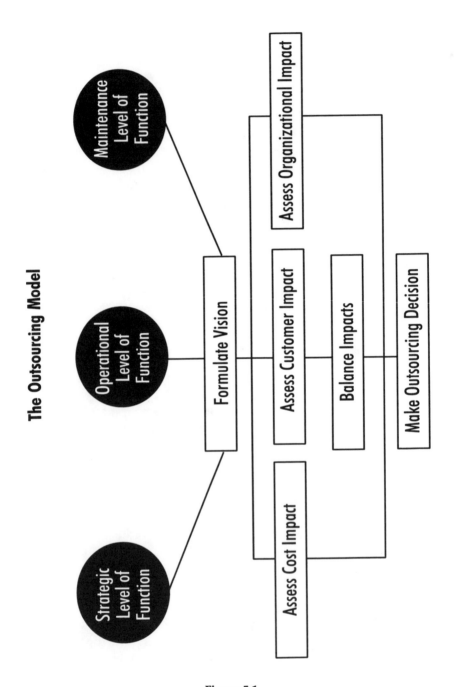

Figure 5.1

core competence to maintain their positions. The model set forth at Figure 5.1 treats outsourcing as a vehicle to achieve such objectives, regardless of how well you currently do something or whether you have the capability to perform the function.

In using the model, we recommend that you consider every function as a potential candidate for outsourcing. More specifically, within each function, you should separately consider whether to outsource three levels of the function: strategic, operational, and maintenance. The question is not whether to outsource benefits, for example, but rather, whether to outsource the strategic level of benefits, the operational level of benefits, and/or the maintenance level of benefits. In the end, you might outsource all three levels, none of the three levels, or some of the three levels (for instance, you might decide to outsource the operational and maintenance levels of benefits while retaining the strategic level in-house). Whatever the result, the key is to break down each function or service by level, so that you achieve the outsourcing solution most narrowly and accurately tailored to your strategic objectives.

The *strategic level* of a function is the thinking, planning, and linking to the organizational strategy of the function. Often times, managers are naturally reluctant to let go of the strategic level of a function. Keep in mind, however, that there are vendors whose core competence rests squarely within the function. Despite your strategic acumen, these vendors may have the research, technology, and experience to perform the strategic level of the function even better. Don't remove the strategic level of function from the outsourcing table just because it involves important decisions.

The *operational level* is the actual performance of the function. This is the level which managers tend to consider first for outsourcing because it represents a way of extending their resources to do what they are asked to do. Don't fall into the trap of automatically assuming that it is the operational level of the function that you should outsource. After all, you might perform the service or function better than a vendor could or, alternatively, you might be able to develop the in-house resources necessary to perform a particular task. Keep in mind that the outsourcing decision must be made to further the survival and development of the organization and approach whether or not to outsource the operational level of a function in an objective, realistic fashion.

The *maintenance level* of a function encompasses all the tasks that enable the operation of a function to continue. It may include record keeping, the upkeep and servicing of equipment, follow-up on operations, or any other task that supports the operations. There is a long history of maintenance functions being outsourced; today, the maintenance of equipment, the collection function of billing, and upkeep of property are commonly outsourced.

Regardless of whether you are considering outsourcing the strategic level, operational level, or maintenance level of a function, the outsourcing model demonstrated at Figure 5.1 contains five steps:

1. Formulate your vision
2. Assess the cost impact
3. Assess the customer impact
4. Assess the organizational impact
5. Balance the assessed impacts against the backdrop of your vision to make your final outsourcing decision

Each of these steps demands time and effort, but adhering to such a framework is the only way to identify strategically what you should outsource within the context of your transformed organization.

Step 1: Formulating Your Vision

The first step is to formulate your vision. It is difficult to move forward if you don't know where you want to go. Accordingly, this is the most fundamental of the five steps captured in the model.

Vision is what you want your transformed organization to be. It is the ideal, the way that you see your organization within the context of the new competitive environment. If you don't have an up to date vision statement, take the time at the outset to determine where you want to go — not just as an HR department but also as an organization, and not just next year but five years from now.

In particular, vision identifies the organization's business focus, core competencies, and core values. *Business focus* is the activities, products, or services in which your organization strives to gain dominance. It answers the fundamental question, "What is our business, and who are our customers?" *Core competence* is the set of skills, knowledge, or activities which gives your organization distinctiveness as judged by your targeted customers. It is the engine which will drive your dominance within the level of your business focus. Core competence is usually present in the current organizational form; alternatively, it can be developed. The identification of core competence answers the question, "What is our competitive advantage and distinctiveness, and through what activities, skills, or knowledge will we achieve world-class status?" *Core values* are the principles and beliefs which define how you operate and identify your preferred code of conduct. An organization that does not have a firm grasp of its values will eventually lose hold of itself. Core values answer the basic question, "What do we believe in and what is important to us?"

By identifying your business focus, core competence, and core values, you can develop your vision. To some, this exercise might seem "soft" or "touchy feely." As a host of leading business thinkers have shown, however, these elements (business focus, core competence, and core values) have a critical and "hard" impact on your bottom line.[1] To others, the vision inquiry might seem unnecessary in determining what to outsource. This is an equally fatal conclusion. Formulating your vision is a necessary starting point in the step-by-step process captured by the model, providing the essential context for all decisions that follow.

In the end, vision is critical because our outsourcing model reveals not only *what* you should outsource but also *why* you should outsource. Steps two through four in the model (assessing the cost, customer, and organizational impact of outsourcing) are designed to unearth these strategic objectives that relate to why you should outsource. Without a clear grasp of your vision, however, the picture

that develops might be fuzzy, distorted, or even misleading. Know where you want to go in the bigger picture
before focusing on the smaller picture of outsourcing.

Step 2: Assessing the Cost Impact

After you formulate your vision, the next step is to assess the
cost impact of outsourcing a function. As a practical matter,
you may take step three (assessing the customer impact) and/
or step four (assessing the organizational impact) at the same
time that you are taking this step. The analysis for each of
these three steps, however, is quite distinct.

Assessing the cost impact is probably the most involved
and detailed of the three assessment steps. To do this, you
must assess the real cost of continuing to perform the function in-house and then compare it to the proposed cost of
outsourcing the function. It is important to include overhead and transaction costs in both estimates. You should
also factor into your analysis the cost of changing or custom-
izing the delivery of the function under both arrangements.

To a certain extent, the cost inquiry involves simple number crunching. Although most HR professionals have
considerable experience with cost ledgers and balance
sheets, you may want to enlist the expertise of your in-house
accounting or finance experts. If you can, present these
experts with benchmarked data that will enable them to
make in-house versus external comparisons. You might
think that you are performing a function less expensively —
but how do you really know without precise figures from
external competitors that perform similar services? Depending on the particular service or function, such benchmarked
data can be bought or, alternatively, developed (with some
internal effort and some external cooperation).

Don't confine your cost inquiry to mere numbers, however. You should be forward thinking here, considering not
only the present but also the future costs of outsourcing the
function vis-a-vis keeping it in-house. Future projections are
hardly an exact science, and you may not be able to produce
precise numbers. Nor do you have a crystal ball. By conducting some research into the ongoing developments of the
given product or service and factoring in the overall market

and economic trends, however, you may be able to gauge the future costs of providing the service or function. This might affect your cost conclusions considerably.

Cost is only one factor and should never be the sole consideration in what to outsource. In this model, it is balanced with other strategic considerations accordingly. For example, you may well decide to pay more in an outsourcing arrangement in order to add capabilities to your strategic architecture. Even in a cost-cutting atmosphere, the goal is to compete on a price-for-performance basis and not just on price alone.

Step 3: Assessing the Customer Impact

The next step in the outsourcing model involves a separate analysis: the effect that outsourcing a particular service or function will have upon your customers. The identity of "your customers" depends on whether you are considering outsourcing a HR service or function (where the customers are the line organization) or whether you are advising another part of the organization that is considering outsourcing a non-HR service or function (where the customers may be still another part of the organization or the ultimate users of the services/products). Either way, the analysis is similar — and similarly important.

Indeed, no organizational unit or department can exist in a vacuum; you have to consider the impact that your actions will have on others. This maxim holds true when outsourcing. Remember, it is the customer's perception of distinctiveness that essentially defines "core competence." In assessing the customer impact of outsourcing a service or function, make sure that outsourcing will not detract from that distinctiveness, will at least maintain it, and will, in the best case scenario, enhance it.

On a more practical level, assessing the customer impact of outsourcing means looking at the improvements in quality of service that you — and your customers — might attain through an external provider. This, in turn, translates into increased capability in quality, service, customization, and customer convenience. There are less obvious effects as well that are equally critical in this new economy, as your outsourcing arrangement could compliment your core competence by providing you with access to additional markets, technology, research, or knowledge which provides indirect benefits to your customers and builds toward the future which you have envisioned.

All of this is essentially a broad inquiry, where you are focusing on what outsourcing a particular level of a particular service or function would mean to your customers, regardless of the specific vendor that you eventually choose. The vendor-by-vendor comparison is for a later date, once you have decided what service or function to outsource. At that point, you may — or may not — include these various factors (*e.g.*, quality, customer service, capabilities) as part of your criteria for selecting the best vendor for your needs and objectives.[2]

Step 4: Assessing the Organizational Impact

The fourth step of the outsourcing model that dictates whether to outsource a specific function involves the organizational impact of outsourcing that function. Here, organizational impact has three components: (1) the impact of transitioning the function to an outsourcing mode, (2) the impact that outsourcing will have on building the organization's overall capability and core competence, and (3) the impact on building the envisioned organization of the future.

First, consider the impact that transitioning the function to an outsourcing mode will have upon the organization. One consideration here is whether the switch to outsourcing will result in delays in service that will not only anger your customers, but also plunge your organization into gridlock. Here, you must exercise foresight in anticipating these practical transition problems; some are probably inevitable and most are probably acceptable, assuming that they are only temporary. An equally important element here relates to outsourcing's effect on your own people. Outsourcing can produce unrest and anxiety among your employees. Again, this probably isn't a major consideration, if the unrest proves to be only temporary. Occasionally, however, outsourcing a function has had a lasting effect on an organization in the form of employee relations problems and poor morale — which can hamper you in the new economy, where you are asking your employees to work smarter and be more entrepreneurial.[3] You should assess your organizational culture and gauge the likelihood of this transitional impact on the front end when deciding what to outsource.

Second, you should assess the impact that outsourcing will have on building the organization's core competence. It has become fashionable to link "outsourcing" with "core competence" and make the interrelation between the two the sole basis for the outsourcing decision. This is too narrow of an analysis. In our model, core competence is not the sole variable in the outsourcing equation; it is but one part of assessing the organizational impact, with other factors in the mix being assessments of cost impact and customer impact. Nevertheless, the impact that outsourcing a function or service will have on your core competence *is* critical. Keep in mind this contrast: capability is knowledge-based and often in the form of know-how, technology, research, market access, and other resources which add value, whereas core competence is the set of skills, knowledge, or activities which gives your company its distinctiveness in the eyes of your customers. A rule of thumb here is that you should build capability both internally and externally (through outsourcing), while you should build core competence only internally. You *can* outsource a service or function that goes directly to your core competence — but you should do so rarely and only under special circumstances. At the very least, you should consider the effects that sending a service or function off-site will have upon your core competence.[4]

Third, and most broadly, you should assess the organizational impact by determining whether outsourcing the function or service brings you closer — or farther away — to becoming the future organization that you have envisioned. This assessment really brings you back to where you began — the formulation of your vision (Step 1). Here, you should make sure that the outsourcing decision fits in with your business focus and is congruent with your core values. More generally, you should assess whether the outsourcing decision will help make you the type of organization that can succeed in today's economy — an organization that is flexible, can compete globally on a price-for-performance basis, has a distinctive core competence that is recognized by its chosen customer base, and has the overall capacity to produce your intended outcomes.

Step 5: Balancing the Assessed Impacts

The last step of the model is to balance the results of the assessments of the impacts (cost, customer, and organizational) against the backdrop of your vision.

Because this is the time where you reach your final decision, this last step in the process is obviously the most crucial in the model. Your vision of the organization is the lens through which you view the balance of the assessed impacts. The systematic approach we have set forth in this chapter will guide you in making the right outsourcing decisions about what you should outsource (if anything) and why you should outsource (if at all) in a manner that supports your vision. Nevertheless, there is no magic formula or governing equation that reveals how you should balance the conclusions that you have reached regarding cost impact, customer impact, and organizational impact. They must be weighed and balanced in light of your unique vision.

This is also potentially the most difficult step in the process. In many instances, you will face a clear-cut decision — the cost, customer, and organizational variables will all point the same way in the outsourcing calculation. Sometimes, however, the variables will point in different directions and you will have a tougher time balancing the factors. By asking yourself the right questions necessary to build the transformed organization, you will at least have the data and information that is necessary to make such difficult decisions. The manager will then do what managers do best: make an informed decision based on somewhat incomplete and conflicting data.

Endnotes

1. *See, e.g.*, C.K. Prahalad and Gary Hamel, "The Core Competence Of The Corporation," *Harvard Business Review*, May–June 1990, pp. 79–91 (discussing the importance of developing your core competence).
2. *See* Chapter Seven herein for a fuller discussion of the vendor selection process.
3. *See* Chapter Nine herein for a fuller discussion of this and other managerial challenges that outsourcing presents.
4. For an excellent analysis of core competence and the relation of outsourcing to core competence, *see* James Brian Quinn, *Intelligent Enterprise* (New York: The Free Press, 1992).

Chapter Six

Shared Services at Amoco:

Maximizing the Value From Support Service Providers

Merrill C. Anderson

In 1994, Amoco Corporation embarked on a restructuring that affected all levels of the organization. A critical part of this restructuring was the design and implementation of the shared services model, an approach that established a centralized group of resources within the organization to deliver products and services to other parts of the organization. Shared services is an alternative approach to outsourcing. It has worked remarkably well at Amoco.

There was, indeed, a perceived need for change in 1994 at Amoco. Many years of business process reengineering, upgrading operational effectiveness, and implementing human resource programs had led Amoco's leadership to an inescapable conclusion: the structure of the entire corporation had to change in order to reap the full benefits of these improvement efforts. The goal of Amoco is to be recognized as the pre-eminent leader in the oil and gas industry. However, Amoco's 1993 financial performance placed Amoco in the middle of the pack of the major oils. It was time for bold action.

As an initial matter, the leadership of Amoco decided to eliminate three operating companies — exploration and production, refining and marketing, and chemicals — and place direct operating responsibility for the 94 business units that comprised the three operating companies under the Corporate group. This restructuring was intended to open up vertical lines of communication and provide greater empowerment to the individual business units. It also necessitated further change, as greater empowerment to the business units placed added emphasis on how these units would operate as true profit and loss business enterprises. The leaders at Amoco deemed it important to provide maximum control to each business unit so that it could understand and manage the cost side as well as the revenue side of their respective profit equations. Stripping out the costs associated with support services, they recognized, would reinforce greater focus on the core aspects of the business. (Support services here include human resources, information technology, finance, purchasing, and other areas.) Amoco's leaders reasoned that the consolidation of all support services throughout the Amoco business enterprise into a central group would remove duplication and reveal the true costs of providing support services. These centralized support functions would then formally charge the business units for their services. The concept of shared services at Amoco was born.

Although the shared service concept is a simple one, implementation of the concept represents a major organizational challenge. Amoco's plan was to consolidate fourteen support functions consisting of 6,400 employees into a single shared services organization. This organization would serve the needs of Amoco's 43,000 employees in over 60 countries worldwide. Each shared services function would formally contract for work with internal business unit customers and charge fully loaded costs for the products and services delivered. No other company had attempted the creation of a shared services organization on such a large scale in such a short time frame. The risks were high but the potential benefits were great.

Being a pioneer in the large scale implementation of the shared services concept offered large financial rewards but also meant that there was little in the way of accessing the experiences and learnings from other organizations. This challenge seemed to ignite the creativity and passion of the employees to make the concept work. Models and tools were developed to better understand and improve internal customer-supplier relationships. A vibrant and robust internal marketplace was envisioned and this vision was the touchstone to assess progress on developing the basic infrastructure to support this marketplace. Forecasting and contracting processes were put into place. Outsourcing ground rules and processes were devised. Information systems were retooled to provide employees with the information needed to effectively manage the internal marketplace, but in a way that was relatively non-bureaucratic.

The creation of shared services reduced the fixed cost structure of delivering these services by hundreds of millions of dollars. Significantly, most people at Amoco felt that service quality increased as well during this time. Making the costs associated with delivering the products and services visible to customers generated some very spirited dialogue between these customers and the service providers. Customers initially experienced "sticker shock" and the need for a couple of aspirin — but soon joined in a focused effort to work together with suppliers to identify and better manage cost drivers. Stronger customer-supplier relationships were forged. Before long, the shared services concept at Amoco was thriving.

But not before the concept of shared services overcame ample resistance. To make this concept a reality requires huge cultural change at most organizations, including Amoco. Indeed, the reorganization launched in 1994 represented a radical change for Amoco, not only in terms of the structure of the organization but also in the way support services were delivered. Shared services employees had to make the shift from being embedded in a business to selling their services to internal business customers in the new Amoco marketplace. There was literally an overnight demand for a new set of competencies — relationship selling, management consulting, market forecasting, and others — that were required to make shared services successful. The culture of entitlement was evaporating. The culture of accountability had begun.

Today, the shared services vision at Amoco continues to help usher in the new culture of accountability. The vision of Amoco's shared services department is to become "a world class supplier, adding value through customer focus, cost leadership, and excellence." An important part of this vision — and one of the rationales for the shared services concept — is to make cost drivers associated with support services visible and therefore easier to manage. Cost leadership alone is not sufficient, however; no organization can "save itself to prosperity." Amoco's vision therefore also emphasizes customer focus and excellence, because an organization that expects to thrive in the future must make investments in its people, set expectations for excellence, and encourage development of strong relationships with its customers. The Amoco vision embraces these initiatives, and its shared service model embodies them.

The Shared Services Model

The shared services model that Amoco has designed and implemented has provided the organization with a way to better understand how to improve the delivery of products and services to internal customers. The model has guided the shared services group at Amoco in creating value for customers, identifying key competencies, and clarifying outsourcing objectives.

A shared services organization may be defined as a centralized group of resources drawn from one or more functional areas that deliver products and services to internal business customers. A customer-supplier relationship is established that makes explicit the exchange of the supplier's products and services with its customer's payment for these products and services. It is the explicit nature of this exchange that allows customers and suppliers to work together, form partnerships, and improve the value of the services provided. The heart of the shared services organization is, in fact, the customer-supplier relationship.

The Amoco shared services organization is centralized in the sense that its component functional organizations operate as cost centers and have dedicated resources. These functional organizations may or may not be geographically centralized. Often, in fact, shared services employees are distributed or co-located throughout their customers business locations. Co-location helps leverage the one true source of competitive advantage that an internal shared services organization enjoys over its external competitors:

proximity and familiarity with the internal customer base. The stronger the relationships that the internal provider can build with its customers, the greater the barrier to market entry by a potential external competitor. Co-location is highly valued by customers, as well, because the desired service is at the customer's fingertips and can be readily and easily accessed.

The essence of the business logic for the shared services concept is to maintain and perhaps even enhance the dedication and responsiveness of decentralized and embedded resources while capturing additional efficiencies of a centralized resource group. The shared services model therefore can realize both effective and efficient business objectives. Customer satisfaction increases as more effective products and services are delivered at lower cost.

The shared services model at Amoco has four fundamental methods of delivering services to internal customers: service center, service brokerage, center of expertise, and integrated solutions. Figure 6.1 demonstrates these four methods of service delivery, which together summarize and capture the essence of how a shared service organization delivers products and services to customers. These methods evoke a sense of context as well as structure and serve as a very powerful lens for designing a shared services organization.

As Figure 6.1 indicates, the four methods of service delivery are organized according to two dimensions. The first dimension is the potential synergy that exists among various service providers that can be tapped to create new products and services. High synergy indicates that a high degree of collaboration among various functional groups is required to successfully develop products or services; low synergy suggests that any given functional group would be able to independently develop products with little impact on product quality.

The second dimension of the shared services model is the degree of customization that is required to deliver the product or service to a given customer effectively. Low customization suggests a commodity product with little (but perhaps some) requirement to be adapted to a specific customer situation; high customization suggests a specialty

Four Methods of Service Delivery

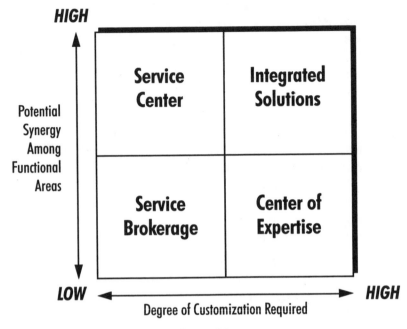

Figure 6.1

product or service that would be tailored to each specific customer application.

These two dimensions largely define (and help distinguish) the four methods of service delivery. The first method of service delivery, a *service center*, describes a service organization that requires a high level of collaboration with other service groups and/or customers to develop commodity products or services. An example of this type of service delivery would be the development of a new standardized purchasing process. Developing such a process would require collaboration and contribution from all affected functional groups (Information Technology, Finance, Manufacturing, Purchasing, etc.). Once the process was developed, however, it would apply to everyone throughout the entire business enterprise with very little need for customization for a given application or functional area.

Service centers add value in part by providing consistency across an entire business enterprise. Line business groups are able to improve horizontal communication and cross-boundary decision making because they share a common language and common processes. Nevertheless, a key competence required on the part of the service provider is to understand cross-boundary business needs and emerging needs. It is important to identify and understand the common denominator business drivers that cut across lines of business. Developing one solution that can be leveraged across many different lines of business can have a powerful impact on increasing business effectiveness and efficiency.

The second method of service delivery, a *service brokerage*, describes a service function that develops commodity products and services with little collaboration or interaction with other functional groups. Service delivery is brokered to third party suppliers that could be within or outside of the business enterprise. For example, if a management training function posts course offerings for a given year, managers would sign up for courses and the training coordinator would act as a broker by scheduling trainers to meet demand, dropping low attendance courses, or adding new courses. These courses would be viewed as commodities because they would be delivered with little customization for a given group.

The primary way a brokerage adds value is by being the low cost provider. Outsourcing can often be a valuable tool in providing a service in such a way that reduces the fixed cost structure incurred by the business. Thus, vendor management becomes a key competence. It is important to understand the needs of a given business, select the appropriate vendor, manage the contracting process between the vendor and the internal customer, and provide regular performance monitoring to ensure that the contracted work is delivered on time and according to specifications.

Centers of expertise, the third method of service delivery in the shared service model, bring together the appropriate technical experts from the entire business enterprise and organize these experts into specialized units where ideas can be quickly developed and shared. These technical experts contract with the business customers to provide ideas and technical excellence to solve business problems.

The desired outcome is to customize a product or service to a particular customer application. Each center may contract separately with customers, minimizing the need for the various centers to collaborate actively. Cross-center infrastructure can be minimized and costs for service kept to a minimum.

Centers of expertise add value for their customers by providing them with customized technical solutions. These centers need to continuously invest in developing technical expertise and in new product development. Innovation is a key competence. Centers of expertise enable the creative energy of technical experts to focus quickly on solving real problems that a line of business may experience. The high need for service customization requires each center to carefully track customer needs, market trends, and technological breakthroughs.

The final method of service delivery, *integrated solutions*, results from the requirements for cross-departmental synergy to develop services as well as strong customer requirements for service customization. Here, departmental boundaries are blurred. Technical and functional experts are viewed as resources who are brought together to meet specific customer needs. Contracting with the customer is done by the team, rather than by the constituent functional organizations. Investments are made to facilitate communication, collaboration, and learning. The return on these investments takes the form of high value added to customers for highly specialized products and services. These products and services often leverage customers' strategies and help them gain or maintain competitive advantage.

An example of an integrated solution approach is the implementation of business audits. Auditing teams would be formed and sent to a specific line of business. These teams would consist of financial auditors, organization development consultants from the HR organization, information technology professionals, and others whose expertise would be tapped to provide a comprehensive analysis of the performance of a business organization. This analysis would go beyond just the financial aspects of the audit and also include operational, organizational, and informational diagnosis. The integrated solutions approach adds value by implementing effective multi-discipline, cross-functional problem solving. Many different perspectives are brought to bear on a given problem. A key competence to enable integrated solutions to be effective is relationship consulting. Service providers need to establish strong relationships with their clients to convey credibility, develop trust, and gain deep insight into their clients business problems.

The Shared Services Model and Outsourcing

When designing and implementing the shared services approach, Amoco resisted the initial temptation to rely too heavily on outsourcing as an option for improving service delivery. There is nevertheless a potential place for outsourcing within the shared services approach. At Amoco, the shared services model was utilized to clarify outsourcing intentions and ensure that these intentions were appropriately aligned to service delivery requirements.

How a shared services organization handles the issue of allowing external competition to have access to its internal customers is critically important. From a shared services perspective, outsourcing service work to external providers may threaten jobs and perhaps even threaten the long-term viability of a given shared services function. External providers therefore can represent a potent source of competition to shared service providers. From a line business perspective, this kind of competition can be very healthy, indeed: the line business leader wants maximum value at the lowest cost for the support services that are purchased, regardless of the source. Outsourcing to external vendors can be a very attractive option to achieve these objectives.

Outsourcing an internal service function is no panacea and is certainly not a replacement for effective and trusting internal customer-supplier relationships. It is, in fact, just another way of expressing these relationships. Building these strong relationships requires both customer and supplier alike to understand how the supplier adds value to the customer's business enterprise. Key competencies required to manage the function must be mutually agreed upon and outsourcing objectives must be established that will capture and return value to the business and provide value to the external vendor, as well.

The experience at Amoco reinforced the notion that it is critically important for customers and suppliers to mutually agree on the intentions for outsourcing. The shared services model has been used to ensure that the intentions are properly aligned with how services are being delivered. Figure 6.2 provides examples of outsourcing intentions that are aligned with each of the four methods of service delivery.

For example, as Figure 6.2 indicates, cost reduction is an appropriate objective for outsourcing brokerage services. These are largely commodity services that can be directly purchased from outside vendors. The shared services model

Methods of Service Delivery and Outsourcing Intentions

Figure 6.2

suggests, however, that cost reduction would not necessarily be an appropriate objective for outsourcing a center of expertise; the work of a center of expertise must be customized to each customer application, and scrimping on cost may run the risk of reducing the effectiveness of the service. This is not to say that outsourcing is not appropriate for a center of expertise — just that outsourcing should be done for other reasons than cost reduction. For example, importing new technology into a center of expertise by contracting some of the work to an outside vendor could be a very appropriate intention for outsourcing. Amoco's internal reengineering practice center of expertise has, for example, hired external vendors to help manage the organizational change process. This has provided Amoco with an opportunity to acquire skills and knowledge about change management and then to transfer these skills and knowledge to the internal consulting group.

For a different reason — to import objectivity — outsourcing may also be used effectively to improve the delivery of integrated solutions. A multi-functional integrated solutions team working on a corporate HR strategy may, for example, contract out an organizational assessment piece of the strategy development process. External HR strategy consultants would be hired to conduct an unbiased diagnosis of the organization. This would be done in order to gain increased objectivity for the assessment. The indicated outsourcing intention for service centers, the intention to increase service quality, is probably appropriate for all four methods of service delivery. Within the specific context of the service center, outsourcing to improve service quality would focus on finding a vendor to ensure consistency of service across all lines of business. The service center would be required to provide timely and responsive service to all customers, showing no favoritism and supplying the same level of service to all customers.

The recent organizational changes in Amoco's compensation and benefits group provide an example of how the shared services model may be used effectively to guide outsourcing decisions. Amoco's HR leadership believed that it was important for compensation and benefits services to be administered consistently across all lines of business. It was also felt that the benefits administration function could be effectively outsourced with the vendors establishing a "help desk" to answer any questions that company employees might have. Vendor management capability at Amoco, however, was not considered to be sufficient to implement and maintain this effort successfully. Plans were put in to place to upgrade vendor management capability through recruitment and development of HR staff.

On the other hand, Amoco decided that it would retain the capability of shaping strategic compensation and benefits planning to meet new and emerging business and customer needs. Creating a strategic compensation consulting capability was viewed as a top priority. Compensation consultants would apply their expertise to each particular customer situation. Therefore, the strategic compensation capability would be established as a center of expertise within Amoco's shared service model. As a center of expertise, this group would need to be managed differently than the compensation and benefits function that remained to operate as a service center within the model. Continued strong investment would need to be made in building technical and functional excellence in the consulting center of expertise through acquisition and development of top quality people. Investments in the help desk service center, on the other hand, would be made sparingly, with the expectation that the vendor would invest appropriately to maintain service delivery.

· · · · ·

Amoco has benefited greatly from utilizing the shared services model. Using the model has effectively reframed the debate from just looking at outsourcing to, instead, one of engaging customers and suppliers to find ways to improve service delivery. Reframing the issue in this way opens up the solution set for improving service delivery and suggests alternative ways of managing support services. This has challenged the leaders of Amoco's support services to become more strategic and link service delivery to line business customer needs. Using the shared services model has also clarified the intentions for outsourcing and ensured that these intentions are appropriately aligned to service delivery requirements. At Amoco, outsourcing is cast as a strategic tool that can accomplish a variety of objectives and is not just viewed as a cost cutting measure.

Most broadly, the shared services model suggests how to better manage service organizations. The model identifies many and varied ways in which a service organization can add value to the business. At Amoco, organizational development activities were geared to increasing the value added for line business customers, identifying functional competencies required for successful service delivery, and making plans to ensure retention, development, and acquisition of these competencies. In the final analysis, the shared service model has helped Amoco become a more effective and more responsive service provider.

PART THREE

GUIDELINES

After you have made the decision to outsource a particular service or function, it is time to turn your attention to forming a healthy outsourcing relationship. Building a successful outsourcing relationship requires much careful thought and painstaking effort on the part of the HR practitioner. The potential benefits are well worth the investment, however, because if you end up outsourcing the right things in the right way, you will meet your outsourcing objectives.

This part of the book focuses on how to outsource. The four chapters that follow each cover a distinct task in constructing and cultivating the outsourcing relationship, supplying practical guidelines that you can follow to ensure that the relationship that you enter into has the desired business outcomes. In Chapter Seven, we examine the process and criteria that you should employ in selecting a service provider. Then, in Chapter Eight, we focus on the outsourcing contract that you should negotiate and enter with the service provider that you eventually select. In Chapter Nine, Dennis Colling of Partners HealthCare System offers some managerial guidelines that will help you transform your outsourcing relationship into a partnership once service is up and running. Finally, in Chapter Ten, Jac Fitz-enz of Saratoga Institute instructs you on how to assess, measure, and evaluate the vendor's performance. Together, these four chapters cover all of the main ingredients needed to build a successful outsourcing relationship.

Chapter Seven

Selecting the Right Vendor

The first step in building a successful outsourcing relationship is selecting the right service provider. To a significant extent, this is also the most critical step in the entire process. As Ross Grossman, vice president of human resource administration for the Prudential Insurance Company of America, points out, "With the right vendor, you can work your way through problems."

Consider the consequences of making an ill-advised decision and choosing the wrong vendor. In that situation, you will not only miss out on the superior service that another vendor could potentially provide, but you will also find yourself mired in an unhealthy outsourcing relationship — one where you are not receiving the cost, quality, or other benefits that you were seeking when you decided to outsource in the first place. In the worst case scenario, you will find yourself in a relationship where there is considerable animosity and little communication between you and your vendor. If you are careful and thorough, however, you will dramatically increase your chances of finding the right outsourcing partner for your needs and objectives. In this chapter, we provide you with an overview of how to find the best vendor for your needs (*see* Figure 7.1 for an illustration of this entire process).

There are two overarching principles that should guide you throughout the evaluation and selection process. First, make sure that you clearly communicate your strategic objectives to prospective service providers. If vendors are unaware or confused about your goals, they may respond with boilerplate bids — and you may find yourself frustrated about your inability to locate a suitable partner. Conversely, if vendors are clear about what you are trying to accomplish through outsourcing, they will likely respond with proposals targeted to your needs. Your ultimate goal

Overview of Vendor Selection Process

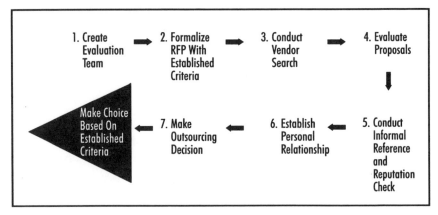

Figure 7.1

here is to find a partner that possesses an understanding of your strategic objectives — and the capabilities to fulfill those objectives.

The second guiding principle is equally important: take your time. As David Limerick and Bert Cunnington have pointed out, the process of entering a strategic alliance with another company is really a period of courtship and compromise. Treat it as such and, unless special circumstances dictate otherwise, don't move too fast.[1] "You need to give yourself enough planning time to make sure that you don't get backed into a corner and have to make a decision on a vendor based on something other than what you're looking for," says Cathy Falzareno, senior vice president of human resources for Builders Square. Make sure that you shop around for the best vendors and conduct a thorough investigation of each before you reach any conclusions, because the stakes are considerable: the vendor that you choose will not only be a primary determinant in the success of your outsourcing venture but will also serve as your representative to your employees and, in many cases, your customers.[2]

Below, we offer some additional guidelines on both the selection process that you should follow as well as the decision criteria that you should employ when evaluating and selecting a vendor to provide an HR service or function (or, by analogy, *any* organizational service or function).

Establishing the Selection Process

Regardless of the specific criteria that you employ in evaluating vendors, a good selection process will improve your chances of choosing the right service provider to fulfill your needs.[3] For the most part, establishing such a process hinges on whether you can establish an evaluation team, formal procedures, and informal procedures that will unearth the best service providers.

The Evaluation Team

At the outset, you need to decide who will decide. The solution here lies somewhere between having the vice president of HR pick the vendor on his or her own and having an *ad hoc* group grapple for some sort of consensus. Instead, you should create a *team* to spearhead the evaluation and selection process.[4]

This is hardly a trivial matter. The typical HR service has many dimensions — technical, operational, financial, legal, and the like. No one person could be expected to master them all when choosing an outsourcing vendor for that service. You should therefore pool the key talent up, down, and across your HR department so that you will be able to make a decision that is informed from all angles. Jane Michel, a consultant for the training and organization consulting services of the corporate human resource organization for Chevron Corporation, believes that, especially for larger outsourcing ventures, it is crucial "to have a team that's put together from the standpoint of differing views and diversity of team members . . . to have all of those people that process information differently and see different things in the world."

Because it is dependent on the magnitude of the outsourcing venture and the culture of your company, there is no magic formula that you can apply to determine how large your team should be. Nor is there an equation that indicates who in particular should be on the team. For sure, the team should include the vice president of human resources and other top executives, both within HR and, if appropriate, from other departments within the organization. Other individuals that might potentially be on the team include your customers, outside consultants, financial analysts, and lawyers. In most instances, the team should also include some of the people that are currently providing the service that you are preparing to outsource. While there is some risk that the current employees, angered that they are being displaced, will attempt to sabotage the process, there are also substantial benefits:

- No one knows the essentials of the service better than the employees currently providing the service; they can provide detailed knowledge that will help vendors submit more accurate proposals, thereby reducing the risk of surprises down the line for you.

- If these employees are to remain with the company after the function is outsourced, their participation in the selection process will increase the chances that they will support the vendor once service begins.

- If the employees are to be displaced after outsourcing begins, you may want them to move with the service for continuity or seamless service; the employees' involvement in the selection process will expose them to the new provider and dramatically increase their chances of landing a position with the vendor.[5]

For all these reasons, make sure that your old in-house providers play a role in selecting the new external providers.

Formal Evaluation Procedures

It is essential that your team structure its selection process with formal evaluation procedures. Without such formal procedures, you may have considerable difficulty in unearthing (in an organized fashion) the best and most compatible service providers for your needs. As June Jones, senior vice president of corporate employee relations for First Interstate Bancorp, says, "We don't just go to lunch with someone and decide, 'We think you're all right, come on in.' We have a very formal process that may be more or less cumbersome depending on how much time we have, how many likely candidates there are, and how much change we anticipate between what we're currently doing and what we'd like to do."

In most cases, this formal process will revolve around a single document: the Request For Proposal (RFP). The creation and utilization of this document requires several steps. **First**, you need to write the RFP. Here, you should view the RFP as, most generally, a vehicle for an exchange of information, where you supply some basic facts about your company and request the same from the vendor.[6] Your RFP may also require vendors to submit a fixed cost bid for the service — although Mary Lacity and Rudy Hirschheim, who have studied outsourcing within the information systems context, warn that this could lead vendors to temper their bids, thereby providing a number which they can back into.[7] Most important, the RFP should clearly and specifically state the level and quality of service that you desire.[8] The vendor should have no choice but to respond with critical, on-point information. "What we want are answers to specific questions so that we can get parallel answers for all the vendors," Jones says. "Instead of telling us about the five things we don't want to know or that may contain the seed of an answer, we want a straightforward, clear answer to the standards or criteria that we've established — do they or don't they have this, how much of it do they have, where is it, and so on." Above all, keep in mind the reasons that you are outsourcing when drafting your RFP. Are you outsourcing for cost, quality, expertise, or other considerations? Make sure that these reasons are reflected in your RFP.

Second, you need to identify potential service providers and solicit bids in response to your RFP. If only one vendor responds to your RFP, you will be forced either to accept that vendor's terms and conditions or resort to your in-house service. Thus, you should try to create a healthy bidding competition among multiple vendors so that they are vying for your favor — and against each other — in the form of favorable terms on price, quality, etc. How do you find such bidders? If you are outsosurcing an HR service or function, formal resources include your local ASTD or SHRM chapter, human resource magazines and journals (some of which print special issues listing potential service providers), and even the Internet. Informally, ask your counterparts from other companies for their recommendations on superior service providers. Jones, for instance, takes a proactive networking approach: "If we know we're going to be in the business of working with vendors or service providers, then it's important for us during the course of the year to find out what these other services are, to get familiar with what they do — not with the urgency of contracting for business immediately ... but rather to get familiar with what the marketplace is offering and what technological or other changes have really revolutionized the way that particular kind of service is being done."

Third, you need to evaluate the various bids that you receive in response to your RFP. The essence of this task involves comparisons of cost, quality, and other criteria between and among the bidders. Your evaluation should not be just a paper review, however. You should schedule a series of meetings where vendors can ask you questions about your RFP and you, in turn, can ask each vendor about the details of its proposal.[9] Through such meetings, you may identify ambiguities or errors in your RFP that elicited inaccurate or misleading proposals; in such circumstances, request a revised proposal from vendors based on the proper information. More importantly, in such presentations, you can start gauging whether you and the vendor will be able to work together in partnership — the type of conclusion that you can make only through face-to-face interaction.

Informal Evaluation Procedures

It would be a mistake to rely solely on the RFP (or whatever other formal procedures that you establish to evaluate vendors). Equally important are the informal evaluation measures that you follow during the evaluation and selection process. Although there are many avenues that you could pursue here, we recommend that, at a minimum, you consider reputation, check references, and establish personal interaction when gathering further information about prospective vendors.

• *Consider Reputation.* In making your vendor selection, you should consider the reputation that the vendor has established in the marketplace. Because we all want to work with the best, you will naturally seek someone who you have heard of and who is known as a high quality provider of services.[10] A note of caution here, however: don't weigh a provider's reputation too heavily in the balance. Indeed, the larger service providers often have the bigger reputations because they are bigger — they can access public relations resources and boast of sizable clients.[11] There is a danger in overlooking the smaller vendors who simply are not skilled at the art of self-promotion; despite their small or non-existent reputation, such a vendor might be the one that can provide the ideal service for your needs. In the final analysis, reputation is important, but beware of slick marketing campaigns (or lack thereof).

• *Check References.* Perhaps more telling is the feedback that you gather from current and former clients of the vendor. After all, the best predictor of a vendor's future behavior is its past behavior.[12] Contact other HR professionals who have entered into outsourcing arrangements with the vendor and ask them about their first-hand experiences with the vendor, particularly with respect to your objectives in outsourcing. You should probe for potential weaknesses — for instance, you might ask the reference to relate how the vendor handled any crisis that emerged in the relationship or how the vendor responded to any complaints or requests for an adjustment in service.[13] It is especially valuable to talk with clients who have had a relationship with the vendor dating back several years and can speak to long-term satisfaction.[14] Conversely, you should not place too much emphasis on the feedback that you receive from recent clients who have just signed on the dotted line and are still in the honeymoon period. Also watch out for the "favorite son" syndrome. "If I had outstanding references from the three people they asked me to talk to, but there's a reputation for not being so good, I'd think twice — because references are hand-picked and reputation is more pervasive," says Prudential's Ross Grossman, who often weighs reputation heavier than reference in the mix for this very reason. If you are concerned that you are not getting the whole story, ask for a comprehensive list, either informally or in your RFP. Cathy

Falzareno of Builders Square says, "One of the first things that we do in a proposal is that we ask them for a client list, and we will go out and do reference checking on our own." Make sure that you do check them, because they often lead to the most valuable information that you can obtain about a vendor.

• *Establish Personal Interaction.* Particularly toward the end of the selection process, you should arrange face-to-face meetings with the vendor where you can interact on a personal basis. This contact should occur on a multi-level basis and involve everyone who might potentially play a key role in the relationship. Besides having vendors give presentations where they explain their RFPs, a good idea here is to conduct a site visit where you can check the vendor's equipment and systems (should they be relevant to the HR service at issue) and talk with the vendor's employees, particularly those who will be servicing you and handling your account. Many human resource leaders make this a key part of their selection process. "We want to see how you work," Falzareno says of the on-site visits she regularly conducts. "I can get a really good feel from the way operations are performed, the way the office looks, whether it seems like things are flowing smoothly, and the kind of time that they give you." Julie Anixter, vice president of training and learning systems for Anixter Inc., goes a step further. She says, "I typically like to test the waters and do some work with somebody — something minimal, something with limited scope — so that we can prove that we can work together effectively, to ourselves, before we would get into anything that is significant." Efforts along these lines should reveal whether you can relate to and are comfortable with the vendor — because sometimes what seems to be a perfect marriage on paper can break down because of a failure to communicate or the simple inability to get along.

Making the Vendor Selection

A good selection process will give you the opportunity to obtain the information that you need to make an informed vendor decision. But what information should you gather?

At the outset, it is critical that you clearly define the evaluation criteria against which you can measure all prospective vendors. There is no "master set" of criteria that is applicable to each decision, as the factors will differ depending on the strategic objectives at hand, the magnitude of the outsourcing initiative, and the needs and culture of the HR department involved. Pay special attention to your customer here. "We ask the customer to help us come up with the criteria," says Chevron's Jane Michel, adding that she often asks her customers to write down "exactly what they want, what outcomes they want to derive from the work effort. Even the act of putting that down on paper or dictating it to somebody to put it down on paper is going to help them, I believe, get clear about what they're really trying to accomplish." Indeed, above all, tailor your criteria to your strategic objectives.

Well-designed criteria can make the difference between a good selection and a poor one. Below we identify nine criteria that are often (but not always) factors in choosing a vendor. You should consult this list when establishing your own criteria, revising or supplementing the list — and weighing the factors on it — according to your own needs and objectives. *See* Figure 7.2 for a sample score sheet listing these criteria that you can use or adapt when evaluating vendors.

1. Cost. It is hard to conceive of a situation where a vendor's price bid will *not* be a factor in the balance. Even where you are outsourcing for quality, strategy, or some reason other than cost, you will certainly consider how much the vendor is planning to charge you. And where you are outsourcing to save money, cost often becomes the paramount criterion that you apply in making your decision. Cost, however, should never be the *only* variable in the equation. "If you let the cost get out ahead, you can end up with more problems than it's worth," says Prudential's Ross Grossman. "You're going to spend more opportunity cost dollars dealing with the problems that are generated with unhappy internal customers than you're going to save — and, ultimately, it isn't going to work." Nor should you always accept the vendor's price bid at face value. Indeed, sometimes the most attractive bids are based

Vendor Evaluation Matrix

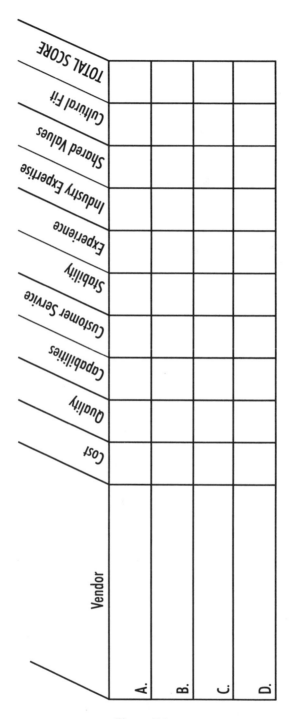

Vendor	Cost	Quality	Capabilities	Customer Service	Stability	Experience	Industry Expertise	Shared Values	Cultural Fit	TOTAL SCORE
A.										
B.										
C.										
D.										

Figure 7.2

on "voodoo economics."[15] If an estimate seems artificially low, make sure that you get the full picture on costs from the vendor.

2. *Quality.* This, too, is almost always a factor, particularly where you are outsourcing to obtain an upgrade in service. With this criterion, you should investigate whether the vendor is truly a leader in providing the HR service that you are outsourcing. Does the vendor have the expertise to back up its reputation and supply best-in-class service? You should also try to ascertain the service provider's commitment to quality, both short-term and long-term. How much pride does the vendor take in its service? Is it willing to take whatever steps are necessary to continue providing best-in-class service for the foreseeable future? As with cost, it is hard to conceive of a situation where quality of product will not be in the mix. After all, a poor product leads to poor service — and unhappy customers.

3. *Capabilities.* Particularly where you are outsourcing to increase your organization's total capabilities so that you can focus internally on your core competencies, the complimentary capabilities of the vendor are central in the selection decision. For instance, imagine that you are outsourcing a technology-dependent HR service to focus on more strategic initiatives. Does the vendor have the systems necessary to provide the service that it promises to deliver or does it plan to secure those systems through a subcontractor? (The latter can be a viable alternative, as long as the vendor is affiliated with the right subcontractor.)[16] Equally important, does the vendor express a commitment to stay on the cutting edge of technology so that you will receive fully competent and updated service not only today, but also tomorrow? If this is, in fact, one of your criterion, make sure that your vendor selection team has someone well versed enough in the subject matter to distinguish state-of-the-art capabilities from mere smoke and mirrors.

4. *Customer Service.* In most instances, you will seek a vendor that displays a strong commitment to customer service. You want to partner with a vendor that will be responsive to your needs, whether they are static or changing, expected or unexpected, reasonable or unreasonable.

Is the vendor flexible? If you are far apart geographically, is the vendor willing to make necessary accommodations or sacrifices? Most broadly, will the vendor make the effort to keep the customer satisfied? The information may begin to emerge during the RFP stage, through the vendor's answers to specific questions. "One of the things I'm measuring [in the RFP] is their capacity to be responsive to a need that we articulate," says June Jones of First Interstate Bancorp. "And so whether they have a good product or not in some cases isn't the first test. The test is, 'Do they read our lips?' . . . If they can't respond to a RFP, my summation is that they'll have a dickens of a time responding to our business needs when we get into the real business of business." A vendor's commitment to customer service may also become evident during your on-site visit. For instance, Cathy Falzareno of Builders Square relates the story of how, during one on-site visit to a vendor, the vendor's executives and employees "kept coming in and going out of that room all day long . . . And I started to get aggravated after a while because I thought, 'What's the deal here? I'm not important enough for you guys to sit here and listen to this? This is some huge business for you and I think it's important that you sit here and listen to what I'm all about and what my company's about.'" She did not select that vendor in part because of such concerns.

5. Stability. The stability factor has three components — financial, leadership, and commitment.

- **Financial:** Make sure that you ascertain the financial health of the vendor. After all, if you sign up with a provider that suddenly goes out of business, your outsourcing venture will fall apart and you will have to spend considerable time and money searching for a new provider.[17] Ask the vendor to supply financial data and bank references; if the vendor refuses, pursue independent channels of financial information.[18]

- **Leadership:** Does the vendor have proven and stable leadership? Will the managers that you are dealing with today be there tomorrow? Jones says, "What I have found to be very helpful in outsourcing relationships . . . is having dialogue with the president or the principals in the organization — people who had the vision to set up the company, people who can listen to where we're going, can listen to the change and hear opportunity for us and for them, and work with us to develop products and services that will be useful to our managers."

- **Commitment:** You do not want to end up with a partner who is likely to leave the outsourcing game tomorrow (thereby increasing the chances that your account will be met with disinterest and seen as an albatross). What is the vendor's commitment to outsourcing? Is it a major — and permanent — part of its business? [19]

6. Experience. When employing this criterion, you should focus on the vendor's prior track record. Does the service provider have outsourcing experience? More specifically, does the vendor have a record for performing the specific HR service at issue? These facts may become evident from reference checks or, more subtly, from the project management procedures that the vendor has put in place for outsourcing arrangements.[20] Be careful in how much weight you accord to this criterion, however. Sometimes, a new entry into the outsourcing vendor market might be the ideal service provider for you, despite its relative inexperience in outsourcing. "I may have never heard of the company before, but actually, the underdog might have a better chance with me," Falzareno admits. "It comes down to the quality of service that I hear in my presentation from them."

7. Industry Expertise. Sometimes, you need a vendor that has a thorough understanding of your particular business. Indeed, the service demands of a hospital's HR department are often quite distinct from the service demands of a similar department in an oil company, even where the same HR service is involved. If this is important to you, look for a vendor that understands your industry and its concerns, pressures, regulatory climate, etc. The same holds true for knowledge of your company. For example, Jones admits that she favors "providers of service who are doing their homework about not only their product but our industry — and our bank, frankly. I like to talk with vendors who know what's going on in our company, who are following the developments of what we're doing and how we're doing it, who have something to offer based on the experience they've shared beyond just, 'Here's my product, don't you want to buy it?,' and who think developmentally."

8. Shared Values. In the end, the vendor that you choose should possess the same values that are integral to your organization. For example, if you value trust and collaboration, you should seek a vendor that values those same things. At the very least, the service provider that you choose should understand what you value and how to behave in light of those values.[21] According to Prudential's Ross Grossman, this means that "they're close enough to the way you view the world that, if there's a gap, you feel that they can narrow it." A similar value structure is essential for a good working relationship and true partnership; an absence of it makes for strange bedfellows.

9. Cultural Fit. A related criterion — and perhaps the most important of all — concerns culture. You should seek a vendor that has a culture similar to yours or, alternatively, can work within your organization's distinct culture. This can be a rather amorphous factor, yet one that is critical in selecting the right vendor — "particularly where their people are sitting with your people," points out Grossman. Thus, when Grossman decided to outsource temporary hiring, ". . . that really involved having someone from another company sitting in our human resources operation, looking like a Prudential employee, and dealing with our internal customers. We looked very carefully at these people. . . . We looked for people who would behave in similar circumstances the way we would." Your definition of "culture" might involve compatibility in philosophies, decision making styles, approaches to problem solving, ways of conducting business, or all of the above. Often the litmus test here revolves around whether you speak the same language; other times, a more detailed examination is required. Regardless of your unique definition, make sure that you communicate your corporate culture to prospective vendors, and then look for a match.

• • • • •

There are no guarantees when you choose an outsourcing service provider. If you follow the right selection process and apply the right decision criteria, however, you can maximize your chances of finding a vendor ideal for your needs and objectives. Remember, no decision is forever; all contracts eventually expire. Even if you are relatively satisfied with the service provider that you have chosen, keep looking around for vendors who might offer even better service. The importance of partnering with the right service provider demands such continued attention.

Endnotes

1. David Limerick and Bert Cunnington, *Managing The New Organization* (San Francisco: Jossey-Bass Publishers, 1993), p. 98.
2. Bill Kelley, "Outsourcing Marches On," *Journal Of Business Strategy*, July–August 1995, p. 41.
3. Arnold Maltz, "Why You Outsource Dictates How," *Transportation & Distribution*, March 1995, p. 78.
4. Mary C. Lacity and Rudy Hirschheim, *Beyond The Information Systems Outsourcing Bandwagon* (Chichester, England: John Wiley & Sons, 1995), pp. 194–200.
5. Maltz, pp. 78–79.
6. "How To Choose A Third-Party Company," *Traffic Management*, July 1992, p. 35.
7. Lacity and Hirschheim, pp. 194-200.
8. Len Marinaccio, "Outsourcing: A Strategic Tool For Managing Human Resources," *Employee Benefits Journal*, March 1994, p. 41; Joseph Judenberg, "Applications Maintenance Outsourcing," *Information Systems Management*, Fall 1994, p. 37.
9. Lacity and Hirschheim, pp. 194–200.
10. Garry J. DeRose and Janet McLaughlin, "Outsourcing Through Partnerships," *Training & Development*, October 1995, p. 53.
11. Maltz, p. 78.
12. Limerick and Cunnington, p. 98.
13. Echo Montgomery Garrett, "Outsourcing To The Max," *Small Business Reports*, August 1994, p. 12.
14. Capers Jones, "Evaluating Software Outsourcing Options," *Information Systems Management*, Fall 1994, p. 30.
15. Lacity and Hirschheim, pp. 194–200.
16. Maltz, p. 74.
17. DeRose and McLaughlin, p. 53.
18. James Carbone, "Outsourcing: It's A Whole New Ballgame!," *Purchasing*, May 18, 1995, p. 43.
19. Judenberg, p. 36.

20. Judenberg, p. 36.
21. DeRose and McLaughlin, p. 53.

Chapter Eight

Entering the Right Contract

Once you have found your outsourcing partner, the next task is to delineate the formal and legal parameters of your outsourcing partnership. Here, the focus is on the contract for services. This instrument is all-important in properly defining the scope of work and performance measures for the selected vendor. Like most other human resource professionals, Julie Anixter, vice president of training and learning systems for Anixter Inc., believes that trust is the foundation for any outsourcing relationship — but as she also points out, "The contract is the contract and, in the end, it's a legally binding relationship . . . Make sure you're not just going on trust."

You need a contract: there is no other practical mechanism that can spell out the parameters of your relationship. You also need a *good* contract because, even if you have found the ideal service provider for your goals and all intentions are good, a poorly designed contract can leave you bound to a poorly performing partner.[1] A good contract may not guarantee a successful outsourcing relationship, but it certainly goes a long way to that end.

This conclusion is borne out by a study conducted by Mary Lacity and Rudy Hirschheim in a different but applicable context. In their study of various organizations that outsourced their information systems function, Lacity and Hirschheim found that the outsourcing contract was *the* key to the success of the outsourcing venture. The companies in the study most dissatisfied with outsourcing had all signed contracts that dramatically favored the vendor. Conversely, Lacity and Hirschheim found that those companies most pleased with outsourcing had signed tight, rigorous contracts that reduced their risks and clearly set forth mutual obligations.[2] The same holds true in the human resource context or any other business context, for that matter: the contract that you negotiate and enter will be a prime determinant of your outsourcing satisfaction.

You should seek a contract that is clear and not overly encumbered by legalese — a document that plainly spells out the roles and obligations of each party. Your contract should also be comprehensive. "It is critically important to approach the contract from the standpoint of the whole project and not to do it in phases," warns Anixter. "You leave yourself open to disconnects when you do it in phases and, although you might not think so, it can get out of hand." As the buyer of the services, you should be in a position to secure a set of favorable terms and conditions from the vendor. This is also the time, however, where you want to start fostering a true partnership with the vendor. When negotiating the contract, you should therefore adopt a mindset that differs from the customary bargaining table mode, changing from a competitive, "win-lose" bargaining style to a collaborative, "win-win" style.[3] With the right mindset and some deft negotiating skills, you can have it all — favorable terms and conditions *plus* an emerging spirit of cooperation and partnership between you and the vendor.

Producing a favorable outsourcing contract also requires considerable patience. Anixter explains, "You have a lot of pressure on you from the business circumstances driving the need for the project, whatever they may be. You have a lot of pressure on you to move quickly. Particularly if you're working on a project that has significance to the company, there's a lot of excitement and enthusiasm and a desire to get going. You're starting to 'fall in love' with your outsourcer, you're getting close, and you're going to make a commitment. You really just have to pull yourself back and modulate your enthusiasm, look at the worst case scenario, and make sure that you are protecting yourself, your company, and the project. When we've slowed down and taken our time, we're always happier."

As when selecting a vendor, your strategic objectives should be paramount in your mind when negotiating and entering a contract. You should not only communicate your goals to the vendor at the bargaining table, but also make sure that there are explicit provisions in the final contract that are designed to meet those goals. Alternatively, you can place your objectives at the forefront by holding the vendor to the promises that it made during the selection process. "Our Request For Proposal has a lot of very specific questions and the vendor responds with some very specific commitments," explains June Jones, senior vice president of corporate employee relations for First Interstate Bancorp. "We normally incorporate the responses of the RFP [into the outsourcing contract] by reference, and in our RFP we state our business goals — what we're trying to accomplish and what we're looking for, at a high level and then more specifically by category." (*See* Chapter Seven for a more detailed discussion of RFPs.) The ultimate aim here is to use the contract to transform your strategic objectives into shared goals. Only then will you be on your way to enjoying the full fruits of a successful outsourcing relationship.

Although most HR practitioners have ample experience with contracts, outsourcing agreements are a special breed. Accordingly, we offer the following ten rules to guide you through the process of negotiating and entering an outsourcing contract and send you on your way to reaping the full benefits of the outsourcing relationship.

1. Set Clear Performance Standards

Fundamentally, your outsourcing contract should establish the service level requirements that will govern the relationship. These are the standards that the vendor must meet in satisfying its requirements under the contract. Here, we are speaking of a detailed description of who, what, where, when, and how the vendor will provide the service.[4]

You should keep several points in mind when negotiating these standards. First, make sure that the contractual provisions addressing the service requirements are *specific*. For example, in a key personnel clause, you might identify the specific employees who will service the account or, if the vendor intends to provide the service through a subcontractor, the specifics of that subcontracting arrangement. Leave nothing to chance or tacit understanding.

"You should be as specific as humanly possible, with the caveat that you will change if necessary by mutual agreement," Anixter says. Insist on a provision that requires total compliance with whatever standards you establish and make sure that you include provisions addressing the vendor's failure to comply with these standards (*e.g.*, penalties). Again, make sure that the parties are specific in defining precisely what constitutes noncompliance.[5]

Another issue here relates to the reporting system that you should spell out in the contract. The goal here is to ensure that you are updated on a regular basis concerning the vendor's performance. In many cases, a vendor's standard report will be inadequate for these purposes. Instead, have the vendor provide you with a report on the requirements that you have established — including the service performance for the most recent time period, explanations for missed standards, and a trend analysis of the performance from previous reporting procedures.[6] You should require such reports at regular intervals — daily, weekly, monthly, quarterly — depending on the nature of the outsourced service. Keep it simple, however, because you end up paying for the time that the vendor spends on reporting and are obliged to keep track of the data supplied. Here again, you should establish penalties for the vendor's failure to comply with the reporting system that you have put into place.[7]

2. Address Personnel Issues

When negotiating your outsourcing contract, don't forget your own people. A failure to do so at this stage could lead to tension and significant personnel problems down the road.

Personnel issues can be a sticky area, both from a human resource standpoint and a legal standpoint. For example, you may want to hire key personnel away from the vendor to bolster your own staff; conversely, the vendor may seek to hire members of your staff away from you. In such a situation, each party may fear a raid of its personnel, which in turn can lead to distrust and resentment — and even litigation.[8] You can avoid these potential problems by addressing these issues in your contract. Consider a mutual no-hire provision, which prohibits recruiting and hiring the other party's employees with a clear indication of the damages a party would suffer if this provision is violated. Even if such a provision is unnecessary because of your approval of this hiring practice, deal with the issue up front — in the contract.[9]

A related personnel issue arises when the hiring of the vendor displaces some of your employees. In such a scenario, you can bargain for contractual provisions that obligate the vendor to provide employment, retraining, placement assistance, or compensation to the displaced employees.[10] You may choose to allow your displaced employees to have right of first refusal on the outsourced positions, although they will be compensated in accordance with the vendor's pay scales. Before you make any move along these lines, however, make sure that you are fully aware of your legal obligations and rights. The sensitivity of the issue demands such caution.

3. Look For Hidden Costs

Particularly if the vendor has a hand in drafting part of the contract, take the time to look for hidden costs. Sometimes, a low price tag may only tell part of the cost story, and you might wind up paying far more than you intended.

In their study of information technology outsourcing, Mary Lacity, Leslie Willcocks, and David Feeny uncovered hidden costs in virtually every vendor-written contract that they reviewed. In some of these contracts, the hidden costs added up to hundreds of thousands of dollars.[11] This does not necessarily mean that your vendor will ask you to sign a contract laden with hidden costs. Take a cautious approach here, however. Review the contract carefully, paying particular attention to incomplete, ambiguous, or open-ended provisions. June Jones of First Interstate Bancorp, for example, guards against these hidden costs by "looking for what factors are likely to influence cost — drive it up or drive it down. And we've also been much more insistent in our contracts about quantifying those fuzzy sorts of additional expenses." For example, if there is a provision for reimbursable expenses, you may choose to place a cap on the level of expenditures, or require approval in advance for costs in excess of a certain dollar limit.

4. Tailor the Fee to the Service

Many outsourcing arrangements are on a fixed price basis — that is, "I will pay you X dollars to provide Y service for Z years." While such a fee structure is often appropriate, particularly where the vendor will provide regular, everyday service, make sure that you explore alternative cost arrangements when negotiating your outsourcing contract. In particular, you should seek to tailor the fee to the particular service involved. Consider E.I. duPont de Nemours and Co. and Corning, Inc., both of which entered recent contracts with service providers for the outsourcing of training. Instead of paying a flat fee, DuPont pays its vendor either on a per-day or a per-project basis. On the other hand, Corning pays its service provider on a per-enrollee basis.[12] There are numerous other ways in which you can arrange cost — for instance, you could make it dependent on volume or tie it to output. Consider the full range of options before negotiating the fee with the vendor.

The key here is to obtain the most value for the best price possible and not simply to keep pushing for a lower price. Such lowballing tactics can, in fact, backfire. Too tough of a bargain can leave vendors financially hamstrung, unable to meet their commitments, and resentful of their new client — hardly the way to start an arrangement that you hope will blossom into a partnership.[13] As Jones observes, "If they cut the price too much, they're going to go out of business. If they go out of business and we've partnered with them, then we don't have support and we're in trouble . . . Sometimes they walk out on a limb hoping for the best but not planning for the worst. And if we know this about vendors, if we know that's why companies fail . . . then why get into it in the first place?"

5. Offer Incentives

As noted above, the ultimate objective in the contracting process is to create shared goals between you and the vendor. Building incentives into the contract can help you bring about this result. "It just gets you both much more focused on the really important things that you want to get done," says Ross Grossman, vice president of human resource administration for the Prudential Insurance Company of America. "Good relationships are wonderful, but dollars also talk."

The logic here is simple: if the vendor has a tangible target that can lead to tangible rewards, it is more likely to deliver a higher caliber service in the hope of hitting that target. You should therefore structure your contract so that the service provider has an incentive to improve the environment in ways beyond merely meeting the baseline performance standards that you have set. Incentives should target overall business goals, including both quantity and quality of the service. Make sure that you set measurable targets, however; you do not want to create a situation where you are bickering with the vendor about whether it has actually improved the service or the environment in general.

In most instances, the inducements here will be financial in nature (although you could establish alternative rewards, such as a priced option to extend the contract on a sole source basis for an extra year or two). You may therefore choose to include an award fee provision so that if the vendor consistently meets or beats the performance criteria during a specified period, the vendor can earn an award fee in addition to its normal fee for services. The extra money may be well spent, because the incentivized portion of the package could lead to extra effort on the part of the vendor — and a dramatically enhanced level of service for you.

6. Don't Get Trapped in a Long-Term Deal

In the late 1980s, a slew of organizations signed splashy, long-term contracts with vendors regarding their information services function. Most of these multi-million deals were for eight to ten years — some even longer. Before the ink had even dried on these contracts, however, many of these organizations were looking for a way out. The long-term deals that they had signed amidst much fanfare several years earlier quickly become worn and outdated in terms of price, service, and/or technology.[14]

HR professionals should heed this lesson. There is considerable danger in entering a long-term arrangement with the vendor. Technology could improve, market prices could drop, or the circumstances of your business could change — and you will be unable to benefit or adapt.[15] Don't get trapped in a long-term deal that might be a "sweetheart" today but could be an albatross tomorrow. Unless the vendor makes a long-term contract worth your while — for instance, with *dramatically* lowered prices in return — seek to enter an agreement of relatively short duration (two to three years, perhaps). For example, Cathy Falzareno, senior vice president of human resources for Builders Square, generally signs outsourcing contracts of two years or less in duration. "We like to be able to reevaluate that process again," she explains. "While that can have negative impact on your cost structure — you have to be really a good negotiator in that process — it's positive in the sense that I think it keeps people on their toes in their service relationship with you." Indeed, you can always renew or extend the contract if you are satisfied with that service relationship.

None of this is to suggest that you should take a short-term view of outsourcing. To the contrary, the most successful outsourcing strategies are not stopgap measures or quick fixes, but are instead long-term in design.

7. Seek Flexibility

Particularly if you sign a long-term contract, make sure that your outsourcing agreement is a flexible instrument that allows for change. Your present needs may not be your future needs — and your contract should be able to respond in kind. Here, we are not referring to the more draconian termination clause discussed below, where you are seeking to end the contract and the relationship. Instead, we are speaking of the situation where you want to keep the contract (and the relationship) alive, but with some alteration. External changes — the type that are constantly taking place in HR today — will often trigger such a desire for adjustment; other times, internal refocusing will mandate altering the contract. Insert mechanisms into the contract that permit you to make revisions or additions to the contract that will adequately respond to these changes.[16]

This may not be easy. In all likelihood, the vendor will refuse to give you the unilateral right to make adjustments to the terms and provisions of the contract (although you may be able to bargain for it at an extremely steep price). Instead, most changes to the contract (if not all) will likely require mutual approval from the parties. If that is the case, the key variable then becomes whether the vendor is flexible enough to make changes or adjustments. Julie Anixter of Anixter Inc. says, "The vendors that we end up working with are those people that are often as flexible as we are and as interested in the long-term as we are ... We gravitate toward those kind of people." Make sure that you have a clause that gives the vendor the option of demonstrating that flexibility.

8. Give Yourself an Escape Route

If you cannot resolve your differences, you need an escape route. What happens if the relationship is not working out as planned and the vendor is not fulfilling its obligations or external circumstances have dramatically changed the nature of the deal that you struck? "We're living in a world that is dumping massive amounts of change on us and we have to be in a position to respond," explains Anixter. "Sometimes the business issues override what was creating the project six months ago, and you have to be prepared for that ... It sometimes means that, 'Well, we've gone down this path, we're explored it, and we're not going any further because our plans have changed.'" Insert a termination clause in your outsourcing contract to account for this scenario.

The termination provision that you establish here will likely be mutual; it is, after all, a clause designed to protect both parties. Moreover, the provision will likely include a notice condition, requiring the terminating party to inform the other of its desire to terminate the contract several weeks or months ahead of time; a rule of thumb here is to give yourself enough time to replace the delivery of that service. Typically, you will establish objective criteria for termination — specific actions or events that give you (or the vendor) the right to terminate the contract before it expires. The failure to perform certain obligations under the contract usually constitutes one such ground; you may also want to establish bankruptcy or the sale of the company as triggering events. Ross Grossman of Prudential goes a step further: the termination clause that he typically bargains for and inserts into his outsourcing contracts gives either party the right to terminate the agreement *for any reason* with a specified, reasonable amount of notice.

However you draft the specific provision, make sure that you include it in your contract. Although the vendor may fight you here and try to lock you up for the duration of the contract, give yourself a way to exit gracefully should the relationship turn sour.

9. Don't Accept a Vendor's Standard Contract

As all the foregoing demonstrates, there are a lot of issues around an outsourcing contract — a lot to consider and a lot to negotiate. For these reasons, don't accept the vendor's standard contract that it might produce as soon as you arrive at the bargaining table.[17] Many human resource professionals are vigilant on this point. Grossman states that, as a matter of course, "We get our attorneys involved and we force a different contract." And if the vendor tries to force its standard contract? "We would walk away, and they know that," says Grossman.

Regardless of how much experience you have in negotiating contracts, the vendor has the advantage here. Outsourcing is, after all, the vendor's business; it has far more experience in negotiating *outsourcing contracts* and has created a standard contract that might seem, at first glance, to be fair and equitable, but may in actuality be laden with one-sided terms and conditions. For instance, the vendor's standard contract might omit fundamental provisions that set performance standards or address the vendor's failure to meet those standards.[18] And even if the vendor's standard contract does contain such provisions, it will probably not address your specific needs. "You need to customize the contract to your individual needs," agrees Cathy Falzareno of Builders Square.

To ensure that you end up with such a customized contract, you can, in fact, employ the same tactics that a vendor uses when preferring its standard contract. Consider the example of Elf Atochem North America, Inc., a Philadelphia-based chemicals manufacturer that recently sought to outsource one of its computer functions. That company preempted consideration of a vendor's standard contract or lengthy negotiation at the bargaining table by taking an unusual step: it drew up its own contract and sent it out to prospective vendors as part of the RFP process. Prospective vendors were allowed to fill in the blanks and vary the terms, but how the vendor responded to the *outsourcer's* standard contract constituted a key part of the decision process.[19] Whether or not you find such an approach appealing, make sure that you discard (or at least customize) the *vendor's* standard contract.

10. Seek Legal Counsel

In today's society, many believe that calling on a lawyer will result in litigation. When outsourcing, the converse may be true: if you don't enlist the help of a lawyer when negotiating the contract, you may end up in litigation. "You have to work very closely with your lawyers," says Julie Anixter of Anixter Inc.. "That's what they're there for, that's what we pay them for, is to protect us."

A legal expert can, indeed, protect you by spotting seemingly harmless yet one-sided provisions. Moreover, a lawyer can help you draft and negotiate the provisions that we have discussed above, as well as some standard yet critical contractual provisions that we have not examined in this chapter (including terms and conditions that address confidentiality, proprietary concerns, disclosure and servicing of competitors, notice requirements, remedies, liability, and choice of law). Finally, and perhaps most importantly, a lawyer can help you make sure that your strategic needs and objectives are adequately built into the contract.

Start by enlisting your in-house counsel. If circumstances dictate, you can hire an outside counsel familiar with outsourcing contracts to work in conjunction with your in-house lawyer. You should also consider hiring non-legal technical experts to help you, depending, of course, on the nature of the service or function that you are outsourcing.[20] June Jones of First Interstate Bancorp, for example, frequently calls upon one of her existing third-party vendors to evaluate a contract with a prospective third-party vendor. Although Jones's existing partner does not have a vested interest in the contract at hand, it does possess much technological, legal, and market expertise about the outsourcing industry in general — expertise that the partner is willing to share. Jones says, "When we put together the contract, I would ask for their assessment about the key categories, any magic wording, or issues that might otherwise be hidden in legal gobbledygook or technical jargon that a lay person, even our attorneys who are specialists in the area, wouldn't necessarily pick up right away."

When negotiating and entering an outsourcing contract, don't just fall back on your own contracting skills and experience, even if they are considerable. The issues are too unique — and the stakes are simply too high — to go to the bargaining table alone. Once there, your negotiations should be guided by the ten rules that we have set forth in this chapter.

Endnotes

1. Garry J. DeRose and Janet McLaughlin, "Outsourcing Through Partnerships," *Training & Development*, October 1995, p. 53.
2. Mary C. Lacity and Rudy Hirschheim, *Beyond The Information Systems Outsourcing Bandwagon* (Chichester, England: John Wiley & Sons, 1995), pp. 200–201.
3. David Limerick and Bert Cunnington, *Managing The New Organization* (San Francisco: Jossey-Bass Publishers, 1993), p. 102.
4. Len Marinaccio, "Outsourcing: A Strategic Tool For Managing Human Resources," *Employee Benefits Journal*, March 1994, p. 41.
5. Jennifer J. Laabs, "Successful Outsourcing Depends On Critical Factors," *Personnel Journal*, October 1993, p. 54.

6. Lacity and Hirschheim, pp. 207–208.
7. Brenda Paik Sunoo and Jennifer J. Laabs, "Winning Strategies For Outsourcing Contracts," *Personnel Journal*, March 1994, p. 77.
8. Mickey Williamson, "Outsourcing Terms Of Agreement," *CIO*, June 1, 1993, pp. 35–36.
9. Sunoo and Laabs, p. 77.
10. Melaine Menagh, "Driving A Hard Bargain," *Computerworld*, August 7, 1995, pp. 69, 73.
11. Mary C. Lacity, Leslie P. Willcocks, and David F. Feeny, "IT Outsourcing: Maximize Flexibility And Control," *Harvard Business Review*, May–June 1995, p. 91.
12. Marc Hequet, "Can You Outsource Your Brain?," *Training*, December 1994, pp. 27–28.
13. Jeffrey M. Kaplan, "Evaluating Network Outsourcing Vendors," *Business Communications Review*, August 1995, p. 50.
14. John J. Xenakis, "The Uncertainty Of Outsourcing," *CFO*, October 1992, p. 75.
15. Lacity, Willcocks, and Feeny, p. 92.
16. Xenakis, p. 76.
17. Lacity and Hirschheim, pp. 201–202; Sunoo and Laabs, p. 75.
18. Lacity and Hirschheim, pp. 201–202.
19. Elizabeth Heichler, "Unique Contract Helps Outsourcing Process," *Computerworld*, April 3, 1995, p. 75.
20. Lacity and Hirschheim, p. 203.

Chapter Nine

Managing the Outsourcing Venture

Dennis Colling

In nearly every industry — including health care, the one in which I work — there is a certain inevitability to outsourcing. It is becoming increasingly clear that less money is being earmarked for administrative functions, including human resources. Staff budgets are becoming a zero-sum game. With a shrinking amount of resources at his or her disposal, the human resources executive now faces some hard cost decisions. At the same time, he or she is expected to provide a high level of service.

Outsourcing is one potential solution here. Like many other HR professionals, I have successfully used outsourcing to save money *and* to serve the organization and its employees. Many human resource people nevertheless remain skeptical of contracting out parts of their organizations because they see it as requiring a great deal of work to bring about and manage without a guarantee of cost savings. In the future, you might have to outsource to get the work done. Accordingly, HR professionals should change their mindset toward outsourcing and understand the rules of partnering effectively and delegating chunks of their operation to outside companies. Otherwise, the outsourcing option will not be viable. In this chapter, I discuss how to manage the outsourcing venture to partnership — and to bottom-line success.

For the typical client-vendor outsourcing relationship, partnership is a difficult but attainable goal. This is not a view to which everyone subscribes. Many HR practitioners believe that outsourcing takes an excessive amount of time and may never achieve cost savings. Others believe that outsourcing service providers can never be true partners because economic incentives aren't in alignment; the best you can achieve is a cat and mouse game with vendors maximizing margins and the HR practitioners minimizing them. It is certainly true that vendors are interested in maximizing their profits. But all organizations (and not just outsourcing vendors) are interested in maximizing their profits. The "vendors cannot be partners" logic would dictate that no two organizations could ever successfully partner with one another. We know this is not true; American business history is replete with examples of successful, profitable partnerships that have benefited each partner involved.

● ● ● ● ●

If, in fact, partnership is attainable, why should you pursue it? Why not concentrate on contracting-detailed specifications for deliverables and tight timelines with penalties? The argument is the same for any other complex undertaking, and the answer goes right to the bottom line. Only through a genuine partnership can you extract the greatest possible benefits from your outsourcing venture. The partnership worth pursuing in the outsourcing arena is decidedly business-like in nature. It is a relationship in which each party works hand-in-hand with the other to bring about shared business goals. In particular, true partnership leads to integration and trust, two powerful forces that can have an enormously positive impact on your bottom line. This reasoning, of course, drives much contemporary management and human resource practice within organizations.

Integration occurs when the two partners — customer and vendor — act as one organization. Traditional customer-vendor boundaries become blurred; in their place stands one intermingled team. Integration is most visibly achieved when the vendor's personnel are providing service on-site, taking part in regular meetings and becoming an active part of the organization's culture.[1] In that scenario, company outsiders soon become the insiders. The vendor need not be on-site for integration to result, however, because integration mainly occurs in the mind (and not merely because of physical proximity). Even if the vendor is headquartered thousands of miles away, integration is possible as long as the service providers are considered part of the group that hired them.[2] The benefits of such integration are clear and considerable. With integration, your objectives become theirs, and each party is working toward true shared goals. More practically, integration eliminates any "us versus them" disputes over roles and responsibilities, producing seamless service for the client.

Trust is less tangible but an equally important benefit of partnership. Although you should maintain some healthy skepticism and openness to review as you would your own operations, partners that trust one another have faith in their partner's abilities, intentions, and integrity. In such an atmosphere, there is no limit to what the partnership can produce. It can be said that genuine partnership leads to trust, or that trust leads to partnership, or that one is the essence of the other. Whatever the precise relation of trust to partnership, it is clear that trust is a desirable result of the outsourcing relationship.

• • • • •

If partnership can be attained, and is in fact worth attaining, then how, finally, do you attain it? The answer lies in strong management of the outsourcing relationship. There are six primary managerial challenges that the HR practitioner faces when outsourcing an HR service:

• Enlisting client support
• Defusing employee resistance
• Deploying internal resources
• Educating your partner
• Defining roles and responsibilities
• Resolving conflicts and problems

All of these steps are proactive and can be viewed not only as "challenges" to overcome but also as "steps" that you should take in cultivating your outsourcing relationship and building toward a stage of true partnership, with its dual benefits of integration and trust.

As you will see, the key to these challenges lies in effective communication. Each managerial challenge requires different forms of communication with different people at different layers in different organizations. The prescription is almost always the same: communicate effectively with the right people in the right way and you will be well on your way to an outsourcing partnership.

1. Enlisting Client Support

Serving customers — employees, managers, many others — has always been and always will be a centerpiece of the HR mission. Accordingly, at the outset of the outsourcing relationship, you should take whatever steps are necessary to enlist client support. This is crucial because you will need to rely on that support in carrying out your outsourcing objectives.

This task alone requires you to take several different managerial actions with different levels of people in the organization. First, it is crucial to obtain the approval and buy-in of the senior leaders for a variety of reasons (political and otherwise) before you finalize your arrangement with the service provider. I have usually done so by taking one or more of the following steps: (1) organizing a meeting with all high-level players within the organization where I clearly communicate the reasons underlying my decision to outsource a particular HR service; (2) involving top management in the vendor selection process; and/or (3) arranging a meeting between top management and my vendor-of-choice where senior leaders can see first hand what the vendor might bring to the table. All of this might require considerable persuasion and a clear presentation of plausible evidence that the outsourcing contract will save money over time and that good service will be maintained or improved while savings are captured. Indeed, top management must not only understand but *believe* that the best way to provide a particular HR service — from both a human resources and an organizational standpoint — is by entering a partnership with another company.[3]

Before service is up and running, it is also critical to pay attention to the concerns of other stakeholders in the organization. Human resources outsourcing decisions may affect other departments or functions — information systems, payroll, public affairs, for example. Also vital are the individuals who most often receive or use the affected HR service. In my experience, I have found that employees are less concerned about why you have decided to outsource and more interested in how that decision will impact them. I tailor my message to them accordingly, emphasizing that they will continue to receive the same high quality service that they have always received (if not better service), pledging that we will try to minimize any personnel problems, and making myself accountable and members of my staff available for any lingering questions or concerns that they might have. The key here is reassurance and sensitivity to client concerns.

Most broadly, you should do whatever you need to do to prepare your organizational culture for the outsourcing venture. With some foresight on the front end, you should be able to overcome potential organizational or customer resistance to your outsourcing venture. A decision to outsource a human resources function can act as a catalyst to develop general communications about the organization's attitude toward and criteria for outsourcing other functions.

2. Defusing Employee Resistance

Another potential source of internal turmoil is employees within your own HR department. Your decision to transfer work from your own people to your new partners may be met with resistance and, in some cases, anger. Particularly if job loss is involved, the upheaval of change can result in poor morale, decreased productivity, and widespread feelings of being sacrificed by the department. Good people may leave. Managing the impact of the outsourcing decision on current staff is crucial, particularly because human resources is a highly visible function in many organizations. To do so, you must deal with two powerful forces at play here: ego and fear.

Ego relates to your employees' pride in the service that they are currently providing but that you have decided to outsource. Your employees may view the decision as an implied criticism. To address these issues, you can explain that your new partner can provide better or cheaper service because it has more advanced technology and/or possesses specific competencies to perform this particular service — and not because it has superior employees. You should also reaffirm your belief in the talent and capabilities of your staff. In general, make the case for outsourcing the service or function and point to the hard business reasons for your decision. Putting this decision in the general context of expense reduction and reengineering is essential.

Fear is even more difficult to combat. Once they hear that you are planning to outsource a service, many of your employees may assume that this is a first step that could threaten their jobs. If in fact there will be no job loss, lay these fears to rest immediately and effectively; be realistic, though, because cost pressures will likely continue to force examination of other functions. The message is obviously different where employees *will* lose their jobs. In that scenario, communicate with your employees as immediately and honestly as you can. Explain that you have made your best efforts to preserve jobs of the people within the department, but that some job loss is unavoidable; if possible, identify the approximate number of jobs that may be lost (it promises to be far less than the employees expect). Reassure your employees that they will be treated fairly and with respect, and answer questions about their employment opportunities (both internally and at the vendor), retirement packages, health benefits, etc. — or otherwise someone else will answer them for you. Obviously, if there is a union contract involved, you must check the provisions in the contract that deal with the transfer of work and layoffs.

Above all, I would strongly suggest that you develop a clear plan for communicating your outsourcing decision to your employees through newsletters, memoranda, and personal meetings. You can also arrange a pre-hire meeting between your employees and the new service provider so that your employees will feel comfortable with who you are bringing in and can ascertain the vendor's capabilities and expertise for themselves. In some cases, your current employees may be excellent candidates for hire in your new partner's organization. After you have taken these steps, your employees may still not like the decision, but at least they might understand it — and that should go a long way toward deflating internal turmoil.

3. Deploying Internal Resources

The next step in managing the outsourcing venture is to select the people within your department who will deal with your new partner. In most cases, this task will primarily involve the appointment of a strong account/contract manager — that is, a "point person" who can serve as an intermediary between users and the service provider, work closely with his or her counterpart at the vendor to create seamless service, monitor vendor performance, and review costs and billings.[4] You should give considerable thought to who among your staff should deal with the vendor at the operational level, as well.

Regardless of the precise lineup that you establish for your outsourcing team, each of the players must all possess certain competencies and skills. Remember, your employees will be used to "owning" the service. Outsourcing requires a different mindset. No longer will your employees actually provide the service; instead, they will be monitoring, coordinating, and interacting with the external company now providing the service. You should therefore select the people on your side who can thrive in a team-based, control sharing venture. The people who you tap must feel comfortable in a broker role, where they are exerting influence but are often, by definition, "hands off." Pay particular attention to managing outcomes rather than specific behaviors. The new partner will likely have a new way of doing things.

At a more fundamental level, this calls for certain baseline values (e.g., trust, collaboration). The competency approach may also work very well here and help establish that internal roles change when a function is outsourced. The most critical competency at play will probably be communication skills. The most successful outsourcing efforts in which I have been involved have enjoyed strong communication links at all levels — operational, account/ contract manager, and top management.[5] I try to pave the way for the establishment of these links by selecting the people on our end who excel at communication to deal with our outsourcing partner.

This is the stage — before service is up and running — where you should make sure that you have thought through and discussed each dimension of the outsourcing relationship. For instance, if you are partnering with a temporary services agency, you need to be certain that you have policies for hiring employees in place, have arranged for health screening, and have prepared all the necessary documentation required by regulatory agencies. A week or month of extra preparatory time is well worth the delay to maximize your chances of a problem-free relationship.

4. Educating Your Partner

Another proactive step that I take early in the outsourcing relationship involves vendor education. For partnership to develop, your new service provider must fully understand your organization. It is up to you to provide the information necessary for the vendor to attain such an understanding.

One piece here involves the service or function that you are outsourcing. Even if you have thoroughly and accurately communicated your service needs in the course of negotiating a contract with the vendor, there exists a strong possibility that the vendor may forget about some of those needs once service is up and running. It therefore pays off to reeducate your partner as to those needs in the early days of service. This may involve providing your partner with information on your technological capabilities, the particular service requirements of certain users within your organization, a restatement of your core values, or any other details that have somehow fallen through the cracks and are not built into the contract. Moreover, you should take steps to make sure that your partner is receiving the ongoing information that will help it to render excellent service. For example, if an outside company is handling your benefits administration, that company should be included in monthly department head meetings and should receive company financials, organization newsletters, and the general stream of information received by internal department heads similarly situated. Such information will allow your partner to provide service that is consistent with where you are going as an organization. Information exchange is essential. The best case is that each party adjusts its business strategy as it gains experience and confidence in the outsourcing arrangement.

A more subtle and probably more critical part of educating your outsourcing partner involves your corporate culture.[6] As James Brian Quinn has pointed out, every organization's culture ". . . has its different language, style, internal politics, and hidden decision rules, which, until understood, exact a high price."[7] The speed with which your partner can understand and align itself with your culture can make or break the outsourcing relationship. For example, my organization recently decided to hire someone to handle the outplacement function. We made it clear to prospective vendors that attention to the nuances of our organization was as important as price in influencing our final selection. Our intention was to contract out the function, not just select a specific service provider, and the partner had to be as sensitive to the situation as we would be ourselves. Once we selected a provider and service began, we made a conscious effort to communicate the "dos" and "don'ts" of our institution, and they, in turn, expressed an active interest in acquiring such cultural information. In relatively short order, the relationship has become strong, in large part because the vendor has become attuned to and enmeshed in our culture. Conversely, I have seen situations where a vendor's inability to grasp the customer's corporate culture has been the chief factor in blocking partnership, even where technical requirements were met. Make sure that this does not happen to your outsourcing relationship by clearly communicating your department's (and organization's) culture —

the values, rules, and principles, and decisionmaking approaches that really matter. Every organization has their "hot buttons"; take steps to ensure that your partner doesn't push them.

There is, of course, a flip side to this: you should make a concerted effort to understand your partner's culture (assuming that it does not clash or conflict with your own). Partnership is, after all, a two-way street. A sound principle of partnering is not only to ask that the vendor live by your folkways but to also make similar efforts to understand and adapt to the culture of your partner.

5. Defining Roles and Responsibilities

An outsourcing partnership requires an initial and continual definition of roles and responsibilities between you and your partner — who does what when and how. While your outsourcing contract certainly will address some of these issues, many crucial details will remain for the manager to sort through. This is the largest managerial challenge that outsourcing presents for the HR practitioner because it brings issues of control to the surface. How much control do you relinquish? How much do you retain?

This is a delicate balance. On the one hand, the essence of outsourcing is that you are paying someone to perform a service or function previously handled exclusively by your department because you believe they can do so better or more economically. For that someone to render fully competent performance, he or she must have the authority to make decisions in that area. It therefore makes little sense to retain a stranglehold on making all those decisions, particularly where you are buying expertise, or to engage in second guessing of those determinations. On the other hand, your department is used to having total control and you may fear that outsourcing will result in a complete loss of control of your business processes and/or resources. A related fear is that your department will become overly dependent on your service provider and lose the capability to perform the service yourself.[8] How can you find a way to define roles and responsibilities in such a way that you retain the right amount of control?

The answer lies in effective monitoring and communication. Monitoring alone requires a managerial balancing act — you want to monitor the vendor in such a way that dramatically reduces the risks but does not dramatically increase the transaction costs.[9] With the right amount of monitoring of the right behaviors and outcomes, however, you can retain the right amount of control over the vendor. Your contract should stipulate a reporting system between you and the vendor; whether it does or not, make sure that you are monitoring the vendor at appropriately regular intervals (weekly, monthly, etc.). There is a considerable financial aspect to all of this. You should frankly discuss the finances of the relationship with your partner, appointing someone other than the vice president of human resources to serve as your financial liaison. Along these lines, make sure that you:

- review the vendor's bills;
- make sure that they are paid in a timely manner;
- solicit cost savings information; and
- tie all of this into the organization and HR budget cycle.

If appropriate, indicate that you will review the relationship and test the market from time to time.

Continuous communication is required to reestablish roles and responsibilities and retain the right amount of control. As Quinn and Frederick Hilmer have observed, the most successful outsourcers retain control over their providers by maintaining close personal contact and rapport at the floor level and political clout and understanding at the top level.[10] The key here is to let the service providers do their job and not spend the time and effort watching them like a hawk but, at the same time, make sure that you are getting what you paid for. With constant and effective communication, you will remain informed — and in control.

6. Resolving Conflicts and Problems

Even if you have successfully taken the proactive steps outlined above — enlisting client support, defusing employee resistance, deploying internal resources, educat-

ing your partner, and defining roles and responsibilities —
conflicts and problems may nevertheless arise between you
and the vendor. Effective communication between and
among all levels (operational, management, and top leadership) not only effectively reduces the risk of such conflict emerging, but also represents the key to overcoming
whatever problems do emerge.

Having a distant, arms-length relationship with your
partner (or, worse, the type where one side feels that it
has the right to pick up the phone and scream at the other)
almost invites conflict. Instead, I try to cultivate personal,
respectful relationships during the course of outsourcing
ventures in which I am involved. One way I encourage
this is by conducting periodic high level meetings on what
each organization is trying to accomplish and the strategic direction that each is pursuing.

There are also less formal means. Business gifts, enter-
tainment, and social events help foster good relations; think
through your policies here, however, and make sure that
you do not overdo it. In general, there is no substitute for
some friendly effort. For instance, I have partnered on several occasions with a Kansas City-based company and have
become friendly with my counterpart there. Every time I
am in Kansas City, or he is in Boston, we try to get together
for lunch or dinner to maintain the relationship. Neither
one of us want to see what we have built damaged by petty
conflict. He would lose the business, and I would lose a
valuable service provider. I encourage my employees at the
operational and managerial levels to try to establish similar
relationships with their counterparts at the Kansas City
company. These relationships act as a radar screen, highlighting potential collisions before they happen. Good communications means that your partner comes to you with
problems early and resolves them quickly.

$$\bullet \quad \bullet \quad \bullet \quad \bullet \quad \bullet$$

An outsourcing partnership doesn't happen overnight.
Much managerial skill and effort is required to get there.
Even with such skill and effort, there is no guarantee that
your relationship will blossom into partnership. Without

such strong, proactive management, however, your vendor is guaranteed to remain your vendor and not your partner. Your service will suffer accordingly. It is critical to remember that, when outsourcing, you can not just enter a contract and walk away. You are still responsible for delivering that service. Skillful, proactive management builds a partnership than can ensure that you meet those responsibilities and delight your mutual customers.

Endnotes

1. *See* Joe Dysart, "JIT-II Rings Up Big Savings," *Distribution*, December 1993, pp. 45–47.
2. N. Dean Mayer, "A Sensible Approach To Outsourcing," *Information Systems Management*, Fall 1994, p. 27.
3. David Limerick and Bert Cunnington, *Managing The New Organization* (San Francisco: Jossey-Bass Publishers, 1993), p. 92.
4. Mary C. Lacity and Rudy Hirschheim, *Beyond The Information Systems Outsourcing Bandwagon* (Chichester, England: John Wiley & Sons, 1995), pp. 211–212.
5. *See* James Brian Quinn, *Intelligent Enterprise* (New York: The Free Press, 1992), pp. 392–393.
6. *See, generally,* Kathleen Correia, "Get Into The Outsourcing Loop," *HRFocus*, April 1994, p. 15; Jennifer J. Laabs, "Successful Outsourcing Depends On Critical Factors," *Personnel Journal*, October 1993, p. 58.
7. Quinn, p. 393.
8. Len Marinaccio, "Outsourcing: A Strategic Tool For Managing Human Resources," *Employee Benefits Journal*, March 1994, p. 42.
9. Lacity and Hirschheim, pp. 211–215.
10. James Brian Quinn and Frederick G. Hilmer, "Strategic Outsourcing," *Sloan Management Review*, Summer 1994, p. 53.

Chapter Ten

Assessing, Measuring, and Evaluating Outsourcing

Jac Fitz-enz

Well, now you've done it. You heard a lot about outsourcing, and you knew that you would only consider it if it would strengthen the competitive position of your company. You reviewed the pros and cons of outsourcing one or another function and you decided to go for it. Then, you selected your outsourcing partner, entered a contract, and built what you believed to be an workable if not more cost effective relationship. Now, it's time to assess your decision. Are you getting what you went after?

There is much more to outsourcing than reducing operating or administrative expenses. The primary reason for any business decision is its effect on competitive advantage. Every firm has certain strategic imperatives which it believes will lead it to competitive advantage. Some have a list of six or seven; some may have only one. Some recent real-life examples include:

Company A: Be number five worldwide in earnings
Company B: Regain leadership in quality and customer service
Company C: Be the lowest cost producer in its industry
Company D: Increase market share two percent
Company E: Be the provider of choice within the industry

The path may be clear and direct or it may be somewhat obscure and indirect; in either case, you are looking for ways to help your firm gain an edge on the competition. In general, however, there are three paths to competitive advantage: quality, productivity, and service. *Quality* deals with error or defect rates and cycle time of a process. *Productivity* is focused on unit cost and quantity of output compared to input. *Service* can be viewed as a noun (that is, a specific act, such as repairing an appliance) or as a verb (the manner or style in which an act is carried out).

Regardless of the pathway, your firm gains competitive advantage as the result of satisfying a customer's need better than someone else can. Ultimately, then, the customer is the key to assessing the results of your outsourcing effort. You might do something better through an outside source, but if it has no effect on the company's ability to serve the customer or on the company's financial health, you probably have not added competitive advantage. Many an apparent improvement project has failed because the end product was not examined from the standpoint of effect on the customer. There are many examples of outsourcing projects that improved a process but added no significant value to the company. Just keep one thing in mind and your outsourcing decision will be effective: **The objective of outsourcing is to support strategic imperatives leading to competitive advantage.**

This chapter sets forth a practical method for assessing, measuring, and evaluating the performance of your outsourcing partner so that you can make sure that your outsourcing decision is leading to the attainment of competitive advantage.

Measuring Competitive Advantage

First, let's clarify our terms. *Measure* means to obtain an indicator, either qualitative or quantitative, of a thing, process, or outcome. *Evaluate* means to make a judgment as to the value of that indicator relative to something. A measure may represent an absolute and visible point in time (ten minutes to ten o'clock), space (fifty feet from the finish line), attitude (customer satisfaction score), or operation (cost per hire). None of these measures have any inherent value or purpose until we relate them to some criterion. An evaluation is the judgment of the utility or desirability of that point in time, space, attitude, or operation as it is compared to the criterion. Ten minutes to ten o'clock may be good if your meeting is at 10:00, but bad if it was at 9:30 and you missed it. Fifty feet from the finish line might be good if no one else is closer than sixty feet from it, but bad if others are already across it. A customer satisfaction score is good or bad depending on what it prompts the customer to do. And spending $2,000 per hire depends ultimately on its relation to your objective.

There are five indicators that can be applied to measure and evaluate the effects of any decision, including outsourcing decisions. These indices are cost, time, quantity (volume), quality (errors or defects), and human reaction. The last covers the reaction of anyone affected by the action; examples are customer satisfaction or employee morale. A simple way to identify measures of performance improvement that can lead to competitive advantage is within the matrix shown in Figure 10.1.

Most, but not all, of the indices in the left column of Figure 10.1 can be applied to measure the three paths to competitive advantage (productivity, quality, and service). Typically, they match up like this:

1. *Cost* is primarily a productivity or service measure in terms of cost per unit produced or delivered. An example would be cost per hire, cost per paycheck, or cost per trainee hour of instruction. Secondarily, it can be applied to quality as in the cost of non-conformance.

2. *Time* has been taken over by the quality people who talk about cycle time of a process. In the service area, it has long been used in measures of time to respond or time to repair.

3. *Quantity* is a measure of volume or sometimes frequency and works mostly with productivity. The traditional output/input ratio shows quantity produced from a given amount of resource input. We can also show the number of people served in a given time period or the number of calls handled by a given number of benefit administrators.

Performance Measurement Matrix

	Productivity	Quality	Service
Cost			
Time			
Volume (Quantity)			
Errors or Defects (Quality)			
Human Reaction			

Figure 10.1

4. Error or defect rate is obviously a *quality* measure. The percent of incorrect items in a batch is the most common application.

5. *Human reaction* is a service indicator. A sample is satisfaction scores obtained in a human resource survey of its management customers. It is also used in measures of employee morale and attitudes.

Building a Measurement Set

One of the dangers of measurement is to focus entirely on one indicator. You might find that your outsourcing program has saved the company money on the process but aggravated employees with slow response time. Their aggravation may turn into lost productivity and offset your savings. On the other hand, response time might be what you wanted, but the number of errors in the work is unacceptable. In every process there are cost, time, and quality elements, as well as volume and customer satisfaction levels. When constructing your contract with your outsourcing partner, it is therefore best to design more than one performance measure into the specifications that govern your partner's performance.

For the sake of having a context, let's consider measuring and evaluating the outsourcing of three types of human resources services: administrative services, employment services, and training.

Administrative Services

Because the outsourcing of benefits administration has been going on for two decades, administrative services contracts have been common since the 1970s. The most popular reasons for them at that time were twofold. One was to reduce the cost of claims administration. The second was to improve service, and frankly, get rid of the nuisance of having to manage a no-win situation — every time an employee didn't get the reimbursement quickly enough, he or she called HR to fix it. Putting the service outside allowed most calls to go directly to the outsourcing partner. Those initial reasons for outsourcing administrative services still hold true today.

The following are a few examples of potential indicators of your outsourcing partner's performance with respect to claims administration:

> **Cost:** cost per claim by type
>
> **Time:** time to reimburse, time to respond to requests for information or complaints
>
> **Quantity:** number of claims paid, number of employee complaints, and the ratio of the number of complaints to number of claims paid
>
> **Quality:** error rate of paid claims
>
> **Human Reaction:** employee satisfaction scores

A second example of an administrative service that is often outsourced is payroll processing. Well over a half million firms in the United States outsource their payroll function. The advantages in doing it are similar to those for claims administration. If we apply the cost, time, volume, error, and human value indicators to the experience we can measure:

Cost: cost per paycheck, cost of manual remakes of checks (time and money)

Time: on time delivery of payroll, time to respond to special requests

Quantity: number of checks processed

Quality: number of checks with errors, or ratio of errors per 1000 checks cut

Human Reaction: attitude and helpfulness of the contractor's staff, satisfaction of employees

The relative importance of one indicator over another is a function of the primary reason for outsourcing. Did you outsource to save money, improve turnaround time, serve someone better than before, or for some other reason? Pick your measure (or measures) accordingly.

No matter what performance measurement(s) you use, make sure that you factor the internal resources that you no longer need into your analysis. When we look at cost savings from outsourcing, one of the interesting sidelights is the question of what do we do with the people, facilities, and equipment that are no longer needed internally. There are essentially two ways to treat unneeded resources: one is to redeploy them to another area and function, and the other is to dispose of them through layoff or equipment sales. To fully understand and account for the true results of outsourcing, you must include this factor. Are the former administrative staff reassigned? If so, what is the outcome of them and the other resources — are we just putting them someplace else because we don't want to terminate them, or are we employing them in some value-adding capacity that might be measurable? What did we do with the equipment and space previously occupied by the in-house function? If the equipment and space sit there unused, that is an expense; if we sell or rent the equipment and/or space to someone outside the company, that is a form of displacement; and if we move other employees into the space or use the equipment elsewhere in the company, that is redeployment. In short, whatever we do, there are cost or savings implications that must be reviewed and may be measurable. *See* Figure 10.2 for an example of cost analysis items for outsourcing payroll processing.

Employment Services

Recently, temporary staff agencies have made major inroads into capturing human resources outsourcing service contracts. There are a number of tried and proven metrics for measuring an employment process. As with the administrative processing of a benefit claim or a paycheck, each occurrence is a project — each has a clear date of beginning, a cycle time of processing, and a date of completion, and each completed project results in happy or unhappy people. The typical measurement of a hiring decision using the five matrices (cost, time, quantity, quality, and human reaction) are as follows:

1. Cost. When one hires using internal staff, there are a half dozen key elements in the hiring process that can be measured. Our annual surveys of human resource activities indicate that there are six factors in the staffing area that account for approximately 90 percent of the cost of hire, plus or minus one percent: (1) advertising, (2) agency fees, (3) referral bonuses, (4) travel of applicants and staff, (5) relocation, and (6) the pay and benefits of the recruiters involved. By tracking these individually, you can see where you are spending your money and react in whatever way will improve your process. In the case of outsourcing, you simply receive an invoice from the contractor, pay it, and then compare that cost to the typical expense of doing it with internal staff.

2. Time. There are three typical measures of time in the hiring process. All have their starting point when the requisition is approved and assigned to the recruiter or contracting agency. They are measured in calendar days, although in the case of temporary, clerical, or operating jobs, they might be measured in hours.

Time to respond: from start date until at least one qualified candidate is presented

Payroll Process Cost Elements

1. Payroll-related labor expense

    - direct labor cost per employee or per paycheck
    - direct labor cost displaceable or redeployable

2. Payroll-related non-labor expense

    - non-labor cost per employee or per paycheck
    - non-labor cost displaceable or redeployable

3. Systems-related labor expense

    - systems labor cost per employee or per paycheck
    - systems labor cost displacement or redeployable

4. Systems-related non-labor expense

    - systems non-labor cost per employee or per paycheck
    - systems non-labor cost displaceable or reployable

Figure 10.2

Time to fill: from start date until the date on which the offer is accepted or, in the case of a simple temporary clerical requisition, until the time that the person is reviewed and accepted by the internal decision maker

Time to start: from start date until the person arrives to go to work

3. Quantity. This is the most obvious measure because we can always count the number of jobs filled. This can be studied further by subdividing requisitions into those filled internally versus those filled externally. In the case of internal fills, we can look at requisitions filled by each recruiter. In the case of both internal and external staffing, we can track the number of requisitions filled versus those opened in a given period of time. The answer to the question of how many requisitions can a recruiter handle is a function of the difficulty of the assignment. An internal recruiter may be able to only handle two or three high level-high skill positions at a time; on the other hand, the same person might be able to deal with an inventory of up to fifty entry or low level jobs. The decision to outsource often hinges on the mix of requisitions assigned to the staffing function.

4. Quality. In this case, the issue is not errors *per se* but, instead, quality of hire. Although the natural tendency is to measure the quality of the hire by monitoring the performance of the person hired over a given period of time, such an approach is problematic. Once we release a person into the organization, anything can happen. It's like a good swimmer wading into a calm ocean: there is no problem so long as conditions do not change, but if an unseen riptide develops or a wave surge occurs, the person might literally be in over his or her head. The same is true of an organization. A competent person may be overwhelmed by unforeseeable changes — for example, the supervisor may leave and the new supervisor may not like the person previously hired, or the job duties may change or be increased beyond the original design, rendering the person somewhat incompetent. In these cases, the problem is not one of hiring but changing organizational needs. The better way and only fair way to evaluate a new hire or even a temporary placement is against the specifications on the requisition form. Every position requisition lays out the job requirements in terms of education, work experience, skills, and intangibles (such as attitude or fit). If the need is for someone with a high school education, three years experience, ability to program in 4GL, and speak Spanish, it is clear what will constitute a quality hire: it will be someone who matches the specifications. In that situation, we can match spec for spec. The other way is to ask the hiring supervisor to rate or rank the new person compared to others previously hired. This method can be applied to external as well as internal placements.

5. Human Reaction. The feelings the person had regarding their placement experience and the satisfaction of the internal customer can be surveyed and compared on an absolute or relative basis. How "happy" is he or she and how does his or her level of satisfaction compare with that of those in the past? One of the major arguments put forth by recruiters for keeping hiring inside is that the external contractor's staff does not know the company or the needs of the hiring manager. This is a specious argument. Indeed, the internal recruiters initially lacked that knowledge, as well, but they were able to acquire it. Any professional recruiter — if he or she is competent — knows how to establish a relationship with the internal customer. For the contract recruiter, such knowledge is absolutely critical because he or she does not have a captive customer like the internal department often does.

Training

Training is now a $55 billion industry in the United States, according to one recent estimate — and that estimate only considered training managed by the HRD function. If training were a company, it would have ranked among the top twenty in the 1995 *Fortune 500* industrials. Still, training is the most "unmanaged" business function. By conservative estimate based on ten years of formal and informal research, there is virtually no cost effectiveness data available in over 90 percent of American companies. Beyond knowing their budgets, most training directors cannot tell you their operating efficiency as measured by cost per trainee hour (or any other measure, for that matter). Worse yet, they have no idea of the impact of their work in business terms or the return on investment of their resource consumption. Given these facts, training is the most vulnerable of all HR functions to outsourcing.

It is no surprise that we are beginning to see an increase in the outsourcing of the training function. There is a barely perceptible but relentless groundswell of support for outsourcing many training programs, if not the whole function. This movement is being driven by converging forces. First, top management has finally come to realize that people — not capital, material, or plant — are truly the ultimate source of competitive advantage. They have thus increased training budgets in the face of uncertain times accordingly. Traveling on a collision course is top management's awareness that their expenditures are rising; CEOs and other high-level executives are looking for an accounting and are increasingly less accepting of subjective equivocations regarding the results of training. These converging forces often lead top management to two possible solutions. One is to put the function in the hands of a line executive who understands how to run a business. The other is to outsource the function to a training company which can provide training and measure its impact.

Whether outsourced or not, it is critical to measure the effects of training. The following is how training and other development exercises can be evaluated.

1. Cost. This can be monitored in terms of total costs of training, cost per program, cost per training hour, or cost per trainee. Cost per trainee hour is the most useful measure since it normalizes all programs.

2. Time. Hours or days of training delivered is the most common metric. This can be separated by skill, department, or level. Examples would be hours devoted to sales, technical, administrative, operational, or managerial topics.

3. Quantity. This third key performance indicator covers volume — the number of people trained in total or within departments or levels.

4. Quality. If you choose to outsource either a training course or the entire function, you should establish measures of quality impact. The measures should be linked directly to indices tracking the three paths to competitive advantage (productivity, quality, and service). They should also account for extraneous factors, such as:

- Skill objectives of the course — people will be taught to *do* something, not just understand a model
- Expected application of skills on the job — what trainees are expected to do (better) as a result of the training
- Observable changes, hopefully positive, as a result of the application of the new skills
- Non-monetary effects — unit cost reduction, lower error rate, fewer customer complaints/higher satisfaction levels

- Monetary value of the unit cost, error rate, customer satisfaction, etc.

It is admittedly easy to see the application of sales, production, or clerical skills. Although more difficult to measure, it is also possible to track the effects of technical certification, teamwork skills, project management, and even coaching. Our work with thirty North American companies in 1993 and 1994 to develop and test a generic measurement and evaluation process successfully tracked such effects. You, too, should demand such a level of impact or effectiveness reporting from the outsourcing vendor that is providing you with training and development services.

5. *Human Reaction.* Although trainee evaluations are the most popular, they are a minimally useful tool because they are normally restricted to opinions or feelings and are not backed by any objective, verifiable performance data. If you do outsource a course, it is useful to get some feedback from the trainees regarding the experience and their opinion regarding relevance.

A sample spreadsheet measuring training performance in terms of cost, time, and volume is demonstrated in Figure 10.3. Other versions of this form could be prepared showing the variables by department, by grade level, or by any other subdivision desired. You

Training Accounting Spreadsheet

Topic	Number Trained	Hours Of Training	Total Cost	Cost Per Trainee Hour
Administraton				
Managerial				
Operator				
Sales				
Technician				

Figure 10.3

could also add the variables of quality and human reaction, depending, of course, on how you to decide to fashion those particular measurements.

• • • • •

Like most other business initiatives, an outsourcing arrangement can be measured and evaluated, as long as you stay focused on the factors displayed in Figure 10.1 — cost, time, quantity (volume), quality (error), and human reaction. Essentially, these factors encompass all business activity and outcomes. In final analysis, there is nothing outside of productivity, quality and service, and there are no activities or results that cannot be described in some combination of cost, time, volume, error, or human indicators. The application of this method will generate the information needed to assess the cost effectiveness of your decision to outsource.

BIBLIOGRAPHIC

NOTES

Chapter One

Outsourcing: A World of Challenge and Opportunity for Human Resources

The subject of this chapter — the role that human resources can play in the outsourcing and strategic partnering that is occurring on a company-wide level throughout all industries — captures a wide variety of readings along a variety of fronts.

Numerous journal and magazine articles have examined the trend of outsourcing in the general business context. Some of the best include Bill Kelley, "Outsourcing Marches On," *Journal Of Business Strategy*, July–August 1995, pp. 38–42; James Carbone, "Outsourcing: It's A Whole New Ballgame!," *Purchasing*, May 18, 1995, pp. 42–45; Robyn Griggs, "Inside Out," *Sales & Marketing Management*, August 1995, pp. 53–57; "The Outsourcing Source Book," *Journal Of Business Strategy*, May–June 1993, pp. 52–60; "A New Way Of Doing Business," *Traffic Management*, July 1992, pp. 33–55; "Try It, You'll Like It," *Traffic Management*, February 1995, pp. 28–31; Helen L. Richardson, "Outsourcing: The Power Worksource," *Transportation & Distribution*, July 1992, pp. 22–24; and Martin Sinderman, "Outsourcing Gains Speed In Corporate World," *National Real Estate Investor*, August 1995, pp. 42–53.

Scores of other articles and books discuss outsourcing within a specific business context. Although we do not cite all of them here because of their sheer volume, some of the most interesting and most informative include Richard Siemers, "Meet The New Outsourcing," *ABA Banking Journal*, June 1995, pp. 52–60 (banking); Deborah Steinborn, "In-House Or Outsource?," *ABA Banking Journal*, December 1994, pp. 58–61 (banking); Stan Makson, "3 Questions Hold Key To Outsourcing Decision," *National Underwriter — Property & Casualty/Risk & Benefits Management*, June 5, 1995, pp. 20, 39 (insurance); Echo Montgomery Garrett, "Outsourcing To The Max," *Small Business Reports*, August 1994, pp. 9–14 (small businesses); Mary C. Lacity and Rudy Hirschheim, *Beyond The Information Systems Outsourcing Bandwagon* (Chichester, England: John Wiley & Sons, 1995) (information systems); Aileen Crowley, "Passing The Buck," *PC Week*,

October 17, 1994, pp. 25, 28 (information technology); John Morrissey, "CIOs Use Outsourcing To Revamp Systems," *Modern Healthcare*, July 24, 1995, pp. 60–68 (healthcare); and Chris Watson, "Why Outsource? To Thrive In An Increasingly Competitive Environment," *Wood & Wood Products*, June 1995, pp. 144–145 (wood industry).

Outsourcing has also attracted its share of criticism. The most theoretical and thought-provoking of these pieces is Richard A. Bettis, Stephen P. Bradley, and Gary Hamel, "Outsourcing And Industrial Decline," *Academy Of Management Executive*, 1992, Vol. 6 No. 1, pp. 7–22. *See also* Paul Strassmann, "Outsourcing: A Game For Losers," *Computerworld*, August 21, 1995, p. 75; Jeffrey M. Kaplan, "Firms Look To Outsource — Themselves," *Computerworld*, June 12, 1995, p. 79; and W. D. Riley, "Outsource With A Vengeance," *Datamation*, March 1, 1995, p. 34. Other commentators are less critical of outsourcing. *See* Stanley J. Goldman, "Creative Outsourcing," *Datamation*, July 15, 1995, p. 84; Susan Scrupski, "Outsourcing Rights Of Passage," *Datamation*, March 15, 1995, p. 32; and Monty Kaufman, "Outsourcing: A Concept With Renewed Meaning," *The Office*, January 1993, p. 50. Still others advocate outsourcing, emphasizing its equities and potential benefits. *See, e.g.*, Peter F. Drucker, *Post-Capitalist Society* (New York: HarperCollins Publishers, 1993), pp. 93–96, and James Brian Quinn, *Intelligent Enterprise* (New York: The Free Press, 1992), pp. 47–55, 74–75. For a philosophical discussion on why outsourcing has emerged in the 1990s, *see* Dernizo Pagnoncelli, "Managed Outsourcing: A Strategy For A Competitive Company In The 1990s," *Management Decision*, Vol. 31, No. 7, 1993, pp. 15–22.

Other authors have gone a step beyond outsourcing and examined strategic partnerships in general, focusing especially on the strategic architecture and structure that organizations have assumed and will assume in the future. *See, e.g.*, Jay R. Galbraith, "The Business Unit Of The Future," *Organizing For The Future* (San Francisco: Jossey-Bass Publishers, 1993), pp. 57–61 (network organizations); Peter F. Drucker, "The Network Society," *The Wall Street Journal*, March 29, 1995, p. A12 (network organizations); Steven L. Goldman, Roger N. Nagel, and Kenneth Preiss, *Agile Competitors And Virtual Organizations* (New York: Van Nostrand Reinhold, 1995) (virtual organizations); Charles Handy, "Trust And The Virtual Organization," *Harvard Business Review*, May–June 1995, pp. 40–50 (virtual organizations); John A. Byrne,

Richard Brandt, and Otis Port, "The Virtual Corporation," *Business Week*, February 8, 1993, pp. 98–103 (virtual organizations); Sally Helgesen, *The Web Of Inclusion* (New York: Currency/ Doubleday, 1995) ("webs of inclusion"); and Stanley Nollen and Helen Axel, *Managing Contingent Workers* (New York: Amacom, 1996) (the contingent workforce and employee leasing).

While all of the above provide an excellent — and necessary — theoretical backdrop for outsourcing, two resources are especially valuable in this regard because of the broad overview that they provide toward strategic partnerships. In *The Boundaryless Organization* (San Francisco: Jossey-Bass Publishers, 1995), Ron Ashkenas, Dave Ulrich, Todd Jick, and Steve Kerr provide a thorough analysis of the new organizational paradigm, emphasizing its fluid structure. Similarly, in *Managing The New Organization* (San Francisco: Jossey-Bass Publishers, 1993), David Limerick and Bert Cunnington supply an excellent blueprint for networks and strategic alliances in general.

Several articles briefly discuss the role that human resources can play in company-wide outsourcing initiatives. *See, e.g.,* Kathleen Correia, "Get Into The Outsourcing Loop," *HRFocus*, April 1994, p. 15; Kathleen Correia, "HR Enters The Outsourcing Loop," *Managing Office Technology*, September 1994, p. 37; and Brenda Paik Sunoo and Jennifer J. Laabs, "Winning Strategies For Outsourcing Contracts," *Personnel Journal*, March 1994, pp. 69–78. More broadly, several articles examine HR's potential role in partnering and strategic alliances. *See* Shari Caudron, "Team Staffing Requires New HR Role," *Personnel Journal*, May 1994, pp. 88–94, and Brenda Paik Sunoo, "Wedding HR To Strategic Alliances," *Personnel Journal*, May 1995, pp. 28–36. On a more theoretical level, Randall S. Schuler, in "Strategic Human Resources Management: Linking The People With The Strategic Needs Of The Business," *Organizational Dynamics*, Summer 1992, pp. 18–32, presents a model for forging the links between business needs and HR practices. Finally, in "Human Resource Management: Building A Strategic Partnership," *Organizing For The Future* (San Francisco: Jossey-Bass Publishers, 1993), pp. 229–255, Allan M. Mohrman, Jr. and Edward E. Lawler, III offer a thoughtful analysis on how the human resources function has evolved — and where it needs to go.

Chapter Two

A Report From the Field

Much of the data presented and analyzed in this chapter was also presented and analyzed in Philip J. Harkins, Stephen M. Brown, and Russell Sullivan, "Shining New Light On A Growing Trend," *HR Magazine*, December 1995, pp. 75–79.

Other articles presenting survey data concerning the outsourcing of certain HR services and functions include Jennifer J. Laabs, "Why HR Is Turning To Outsourcing," *Personnel Journal*, September 1993, pp. 92–101 (discussing survey data from Hewitt Associates concerning the benefits function); Sue Burzawa, "Benefits Outsourcing Evolves To Meet Human Resources Challenges And Changes," *Employee Benefit Plan Review*, July 1994, pp. 36–37 (presenting survey data from Foster Higgins concerning the benefits function); "Execs Use Outsourcing, Technology To Run HR Departments," *Employee Benefit Plan Review*, November 1993, pp. 22–24 (same); Miriam Basch Scott, "Outsourcing Affords Employers Improved Administration, Benefits," *Employee Benefit Plan Review*, November 1994, pp. 44–45 (discussing survey data from Wyatt Data Services, Inc. concerning human resource and benefits functions); and "Outsourcing Trend Continues For Benefits Administration," *HRFocus*, April 1995, p. 6 (discussing survey data from the Alexander Consulting Group concerning the benefits function).

There are several other articles in human resource journals or magazines that do not present any data but offer an excellent analysis of the phenomenon of outsourcing human resource services and functions. Perhaps the best and most insightful of these articles is James C. Spee, "Addition By Subtraction," *HR Magazine*, March 1995, pp. 38–43 (also briefly referencing survey data). In "Successful Outsourcing Depends On Critical Factors," *Personnel Journal*, October 1993, pp. 51–60, Jennifer J. Laabs examines the practice and offers guidelines on how to do it well. Len Marinaccio takes a similar approach in "Outsourcing: A Strategic Tool For Managing Human Resources," *Employee Benefits Journal*, March 1994, pp. 39–42, as does Sandra E. O'Connell in "Outsourcing: A Technology-Based Decision," *HR Magazine*, February 1995, pp. 35–39, albeit with an emphasis on computers and data systems.

Other articles focus on a particular service or function in discussing the phenomenon of outsourcing within the context of human resources. *See, e.g.,* Garry J. DeRose and Janet McLaughlin, "Outsourcing Through Partnerships," *Training & Development,* October 1995, pp. 51–55 (training); Marc Hequet, "Can You Outsource Your Brain?," *Training,* December 1994, pp. 27–30 (training); Margaret Kaeter, "An Outsourcing Primer," *Training & Development,* November 1995, pp. 20–25 (training); William M. Craft, "Partner With Your Local Community College," *HRFocus,* April 1995, p. 22 (training); Anita Bruzzese, "Outsourcing Relocation," *Human Resource Executive,* August 1994, pp. 27–29 (relocation); Bill Leonard, "Outsourcing Relocation Services — Are HR Managers Cutting Their Own Throats?," *HR Magazine,* December 1993, pp. 57–58 (relocation); Edward G. Pringle, "The Advantages Of Benefits Outsourcing," *Risk Management,* July 1995, pp. 61–64 (benefits); and Eric Raimy, "Here Today, Outsourced Tomorrow," *Human Resource Executive,* March 1993, pp. 22–25 (temporary services).

Finally, for a contextual view concerning where outsourcing fits in with the other developments and movements impacting human resources, *see* Marlene L. Morgenstern, "The Board's Perspective: Compensation And The New Employment Relationship," *Compensation & Benefits Review,* March–April 1995, pp. 37–44.

Chapter Three

Outsourcing and the Enterprise Value Chain

Several resources offer brief yet revealing analyses of value chains within the context of the new organizational architecture and design. Especially noteworthy here is James Brian Quinn, *Intelligent Enterprise* (New York: The Free Press, 1992), which touches upon outsourcing's relation to the value chain and also contains a superb overview on the way in which organizations are moving towards becoming knowledge enterprises. *See also* Ron Ashkenas, Dave Ulrich, Todd Jick, and Steve Kerr, *The Boundaryless Organization* (San Francisco: Jossey-Bass Publishers, 1995), pp. 192–204 (offering a brief yet illuminating discussion of value chains within the context of the boundaryless organization).

This chapter references several other strains of research that relate to its subject matter. The Corporate Leadership Council's recent report, *Vision Of The Future: Role Of Human Resources In The New Corporate Headquarters* (New York: Corporate Leadership Council, 1995) contains numerous conclusions on the actual and potential importance of human resources in the corporate setting and recommendations for moving human resources into the era of human capital management. The research findings of Drs. Mark A. Huselid and Brian E. Becker relating to the relationship between human resource management and organizational performance are summarized in Mark A. Huselid and Brian E. Becker, "The Strategic Impact Of Human Resources: Building High Performance Work Systems," *hr advisory*, Summer 1995, pp. 2–6. Finally, for a more detailed explanation of SunTrust's outsourcing decision, *see* Lane Caruso and Lee Mulert, "Outsourcing — The Decision," *hr advisory*, Winter 1996, pp. 2–4.

Chapter Four

Market Dynamics and the Future of HR Outsourcing

Most of the literature that addresses the topic of this chapter — the future of human resources outsourcing — predicts that outsourcing will remain a prevalent practice within HR in the coming years. In "Trend Analysis: Know What's Happening Before It Happens," *HRFocus*, March 1995, pp. 1, 4–5, Donald J. McNerney predicts that outsourcing will continue to grow in the course of listing the key trends affecting HR. One consultant reaches a similar conclusion — particularly with respect to benefits — in "Who Will Do The Work: Benefits, Outsourcing, And The Employment Contract," *Employee Benefit Plan Review*, July 1995, pp. 10–12. In "Human Resource Management: Building A Strategic Partnership," *Organizing For The Future* (San Francisco: Jossey-Bass Publishers, 1993), p. 250, Allan M. Mohrman, Jr. and Edward E. Lawler, III forecast that human resource managers will continue to contract out responsibilities for a variety of reasons. *See also* Philip J. Harkins, Stephen M. Brown, and Russell Sullivan, "Shining New Light On A Growing Trend," *HR Magazine*, December 1995, pp. 75–79 (predicting that outsourcing is not a fad and is here to stay) and Chapter One herein. Other articles addressing the future of HR outsourcing in a more non-committal fashion include Jennifer J. Laabs, "Why HR Is Turning To Outsourcing," *Personnel Journal*, September 1993, pp. 92–101, and Marc Hequet, "Can You Outsource Your Brain?," *Training*, December 1994, pp. 27–30.

Within the overall business context, several authors offers predictions on the future of outsourcing. Most see the practice continuing or increasing. *See, e.g.*, Richard A. Jacobs, "The Invisible Workforce: How To Align Contract And Temporary Workers With Core Organizational Goals," *National Productivity Review*, Spring 1994, pp. 181–182 (observing that "[i]t is difficult to envision a successful company in the twenty–first century that does not have a contract management effort"), and Mary C. Lacity and Rudy Hirschheim, *Beyond The Information Systems Outsourcing Bandwagon* (Chichester, England: John Wiley & Sons, 1995), pp. 225–226 (predicting that there will be an increased number of vendors and vendor offerings, as well as shorter and tighter contracts, within the context of information systems).

Chapter Five

A Strategic Approach to Outsourcing

A condensed version of the model set forth in this chapter is included in Philip J. Harkins, Stephen M. Brown, and Russell Sullivan, "Shining New Light On A Growing Trend," *HR Magazine*, December 1995, pp. 75–79. Other articles in human resource journals or magazines that set forth an approach, model, or guidelines that indicate what HR service or function to outsource (and/or why to outsource) include Len Marinaccio, "Outsourcing: A Strategic Tool For Managing Human Resources," *Employee Benefits Journal*, March 1994, pp. 39–42; Sandra E. O'Connell, "Outsourcing: A Technology-Based Decision," *HR Magazine*, February 1995, pp. 35–39; and Jennifer J. Laabs, "Successful Outsourcing Depends On Critical Factors," *Personnel Journal*, October 1993, pp. 51–60.

Equally important are the approaches and models contained in the general, "non-HR" literature that are useful to the HR professional by analogy. In *Intelligent Enterprise* (New York: The Free Press, 1992), James Brian Quinn sets forth a well-reasoned approach to outsourcing that revolves around the concept of core competencies. *See also* James Brian Quinn and Frederick G. Hilmer, "Strategic Outsourcing," *Sloan Management Review*, Summer 1994, pp. 43–55. Similarly, Mary C. Lacity and Rudy Hirschheim present a step-by-step approach to what they term "selective sourcing" in *Beyond The Information Systems Outsourcing Bandwagon* (Chichester, England: John Wiley & Sons, 1995), pp. 175–216, 223–224. *See also* Mary C. Lacity, Leslie P. Willcocks, and David F. Feeny, "IT Outsourcing: Maximize Flexibility And Control," *Harvard Business Review*, May–June 1995, pp. 84–93 (similarly advocating selective outsourcing), and Mary Lacity, Rudy Hirschheim, and Leslie Willcocks, "Realizing Outsourcing Expectations," *Information Systems Management*, Fall 1994, pp. 7–18 (same).

For other approaches and/or models relating to outsourcing, *see* Ravi Venkatesan, "Strategic Sourcing: To Make Or Not To Make," *Harvard Business Review*, November–December 1992, pp. 98–107; James A. Welch and P. Ranganath Nayak, "Strategic Sourcing: A Progressive Approach To The Make-Or-Buy Decision," *Academy Of Management Executive*, 1992, Vol. 6 No. 1, pp. 23–31; Richard A. Jacobs, "The Invisible Workforce: How To Align Contract And Temporary Workers With Core Organizational Goals," *National Productivity Review*, Spring 1994, pp. 169–183; and Dernizo Pagnoncelli, "Managed Outsourcing: A Strategy For A Competitive Company In The 1990s," *Management Decision*, Vol. 31, No. 7, 1993, pp. 15–22.

This chapter also introduces the idea of the transformed organization. For some other views on what organizations must do to remain competitive in the 1990s, *see* Dave Ulrich and Dale Lake, *Organizational Capability* (New York: John Wiley & Sons, 1990); Ralph H. Killman, Ines Killman, and Associates, *Making Organizations Competitive* (San Francisco: Jossey-Bass Publishers, 1991); and Peter F. Drucker, *Post-Capitalist Society* (New York: HarperCollins Publishers, 1993). For an outstanding and concise analysis of the importance of core competence to organizational success, *see* C.K. Prahalad and Gary Hamel, "The Core Competence Of The Corporation," *Harvard Business Review*, May–June 1990, pp. 79–91.

Chapter Six

Shared Services at Amoco: Maximizing the Value From Support Service Providers

Shared services is a relatively new concept, and the literature on it is accordingly sparse. Nevertheless, for an outstanding overview of the concept, an analysis of its strengths, and some guidelines on how to implement it, *see* Ron Ashkenas, Dave Ulrich, Todd Jick, and Steve Kerr, *The Boundaryless Organization* (San Francisco: Jossey-Bass Publishers 1995), pp. 168–176.

For other alternative approaches and/or models to outsourcing, *see* Mary C. Lacity and Rudy Hirschheim, *Beyond The Information Systems Outsourcing Bandwagon* (Chichester, England: John Wiley & Sons, 1995) (discussing the "insourcing" option), and Stanley Nollen and Helen Axel, *Managing Contingent Workers* (New York: Amacam, 1996), pp. 40–53 (setting forth a step-by-step approach to making intelligent choices about a contingent workforce).

Chapter Seven

Selecting the Right Vendor

Although no resource treats the issue of selecting a vendor in depth within the context of human resources, several articles in human resource journals and magazines set forth some opinions and guidelines on the subject. In "Winning Strategies For Outsourcing Contracts," *Personnel Journal*, March 1994, pp. 69–78, Brenda Paik Sunoo and Jennifer J. Laabs discuss the necessity of initiating an aggressive bidding process among vendors. James C. Spee, in "Addition By Subtraction," *HR Magazine*, March 1995, pp. 38–43, focuses upon how to identify potentially qualified service providers, while Garry J. DeRose and Janet McLaughlin detail the selection process and criteria that Corning used in outsourcing its training function in "Outsourcing Through Partnerships," *Training & Development*, October 1995, pp. 51–55. Other articles offering guidelines for selecting a vendor within the HR context include Len Marinaccio, "Outsourcing: A Strategic Tool For Managing Human Resources," *Employee Benefits Journal*, March 1994, pp. 39–42; Anita Bruzzese, "Outsourcing Relocation," *Human Resource Executive*, August 1994, pp. 27–29; Mitch Meisler, "Outsourcing Customer Communications Reduces Cost, Improves Timeliness," *Managing Office Technology*, May 1995, pp. 31–32; and Margaret Kaeter, "An Outsourcing Primer," *Training & Development*, November 1995, pp. 20–25.

Within the related information systems context, Mary C. Lacity and Rudy Hirschheim offer a fairly comprehensive treatment of the vendor selection process, particularly with respect to RFPs, in *Beyond The Information Systems Outsourcing Bandwagon* (Chichester, England: John Wiley & Sons, 1995), pp. 194–200. In "Applications Maintenance Outsourcing," *Information Systems Management*, Fall 1994, pp. 34–38, Joseph Judenberg offers some excellent guidelines for selecting an IS service provider; the same holds true for a companion article, Capers Jones, "Evaluating Software Outsourcing Options," *Information Systems Management*, Fall 1994, pp. 28–33. *See also* Mary C. Lacity, Leslie P. Willcocks, and David F. Feeny, "IT Outsourcing: Maximize Flexibility And Control," *Harvard Business Review*, May–June 1995, pp. 84–93, and John Cross, "IT Outsourcing: British Petroleum's Competitive Approach," *Harvard Business Review*, May–June 1995, pp. 94–102 (each discussing an outsourcing approach that fosters competition among multiple suppliers). *But see also* Felix Brück, "Make Versus Buy: The Wrong Decisions Cost," *The McKinsey Quarterly*, 1995 Number 1, pp. 28–47 (examining the advantages of having a sole supplier), and Peter Hines, "Network Sourcing: A Hybrid Approach," *International Journal Of Purchasing And Materials Management*, Spring 1995, pp. 18–24 (comparing "single sourcing" to "multiple sourcing" and championing a hybrid approach, "network sourcing").

Numerous authors have discussed selecting an outsourcing vendor in contexts other than HR or IS, and many offer tips that are useful by analogy. Some of the best articles in this regard include Arnold Maltz, "Why You Outsource Dictates How," *Transportation & Distribution*, March 1995, pp. 73–80 (contract logistics); "How To Choose A Third-Party Company," *Traffic Management*, July 1992, pp. 34–35 (same); James Carbone, "Outsourcing: It's A

Whole New Ballgame!," *Purchasing*, May 18, 1995, pp. 42–45 (contract manufacturing); David Stahl, "Awaiting The Handshake," *Savings & Community Banker*, November 1994, pp. 12–18 (banking); Aileen Crowley, "Build Your Partnership On Solid Ground," *PC Week*, October 17, 1994, p. 32 (computers); Echo Montgomery Garrett, "Outsourcing To The Max," *Small Business Reports*, August 1994, pp. 9–14 (small businesses); and Bill Kelley, "Outsourcing Marches On," *Journal Of Business Strategy*, July–August 1995, pp. 38–42 (general business).

More generally, *see* "How To Be The Winning Bidder," *Agency Sales Magazine*, October 1993, pp. 27–28 for a vendor's perspective on the bidding process and David Limerick and Bert Cunnington, *Managing The New Organization* (San Francisco: Jossey-Bass Publishers, 1993), pp. 87–111 for some overarching principles on managing networks and establishing strategic alliances.

Chapter Eight

Entering the Right Contract

The most pertinent resource on outsourcing contracts within the HR context is Brenda Paik Sunoo and Jennifer J. Laabs, "Winning Strategies For Outsourcing Contracts," *Personnel Journal*, March 1994, pp. 69–78. In that article, the authors make a number of recommendations concerning the negotiation and formation of the outsourcing contract, supporting their views with anecdotes from the field and research conducted by Mary C. Lacity and Rudy Hirschheim in the information systems context. Indeed, Lacity and Hirschheim's most recent work, *Beyond the Information Systems Outsourcing Bandwagon* (Chichester, England: John Wiley & Sons, 1995), pp. 200–211, contains a lengthy and useful discussion on outsourcing contracts. *See also* Mary C. Lacity, Leslie P. Willcocks, and David F. Feeny, "IT Outsourcing: Maximize Flexibility And Control," *Harvard Business Review*, May–June 1995, pp. 84–93 (offering additional tips on the contracting process).

There are several additional journal articles on contracts that address the outsourcing of HR services. In "Successful Outsourcing Depends On Critical Factors," *Personnel Journal*, October 1993, pp. 51–60, Jennifer J. Laabs identifies some broad concerns that might underlie your bargaining table strategy, while in "Outsourcing: A Strategic Tool For Managing Human Resources," *Employee Benefits Journal*, March 1994, pp. 39–42, Len Marinaccio briefly addresses the need for a tight, flexible outsourcing contract. Two additional articles touch upon the specific outsourcing contracts negotiated by specific organizations concerning the outsourcing of the training function. *See* Garry J. DeRose and Janet McLaughlin, "Outsourcing Through Partnerships," *Training & Development*, October 1995, pp. 51–55 (discussing an outsourcing contract negotiated by Corning) and Marc Hequet, "Can You Outsource Your Brain?," *Training*, December 1994, pp. 27–30 (discussing outsourcing contracts negotiated by Corning and DuPont). *See also* Allan M. Mohrman, Jr. and Edward E. Lawler, III, "Human Resource Management: Building A Strategic Partnership," *Organizing For The Future* (San Francisco: Jossey-Bass Publishers, 1993), pp. 253–254 (discussing the present and future challenges of contract negotiation for human resource managers).

There are a number of articles outside the HR context offering guidelines on outsourcing contracts that are useful to the HR practitioner by analogy. Particularly noteworthy here is Mickey Williamson, "Outsourcing Terms Of Agreement," *CIO*, June 1, 1993, pp. 30–36 (setting forth a variety of issues to consider during negotiation), and John J. Xenakis, "The Uncertainty Of Outsourcing," *CFO*, October 1992, pp. 75–76 (identifying critical lessons that companies learned in the IS context with respect to flexibility and the length of contracts). Other articles providing practical contracting tips along these lines include Joseph Judenberg, "Applications Maintenance Outsourcing," *Information Systems Management*, Fall 1994, pp. 34–38; Alfred C. Kellogg, "An Outsourcing Deal Shouldn't Be A Straitjacket," *American Banker*, July 6, 1995, p.18; Jeff Moad, "Outsourcing? Go Out On The Limb Together," *Datamation*, February 1, 1995, pp. 58–61; Gail Greenspan, "Write Tight IT Services Contracts," *Datamation*, August 1, 1995, p. 84; and Melanie Menagh, "Driving A Hard Bargain," *Computerworld*, August 7, 1995, pp. 69, 73, 76.

For conflicting viewpoints on the value of lawyers with respect to HR, *see* Susan Scrupski, "Don't Shoot All The Lawyers," *Datamation*, October 15, 1994, p. 36 (advocating the use of counsel during the outsourcing contract process), and Dr. M. Michael Markowich, "Who's Running HR? Attorneys?," *Personnel Journal*,

May 1994, p. 150 (bemoaning HR's general reliance on attorneys). Finally, for the change in mindset that needs to take place when negotiating a contract with a potential partner and other broad partnership concerns, *see* David Limerick and Bert Cunnington, *Managing the New Organization* (San Francisco: Jossey-Bass Publishers, 1993), pp. 87–111.

Chapter Nine

Managing the Outsourcing Venture

The literature on managing the outsourcing relationship within the human resources context is sparse yet valuable. Allan M. Mohrman, Jr. and Edward E. Lawler, III, "Human Resource Management: Building A Stragetic Partnership," *Organizing For The Future* (San Francisco: Jossey-Bass Publishers, 1993), pp. 249–252, provide an insightful overview of the managerial challenges facing HR when outsourcing. In "Outsourcing Through Partnerships," *Training & Development*, October 1995, pp. 51–55, Garry J. DeRose and Janet McLaughlin reveal how Corning managed its outsourcing venture with its outside provider of training services. Jennifer J. Laabs, in "Successful Outsourcing Depends On Critical Factors," *Personnel Journal,* October 1993, pp. 51–60, discusses how to manage issues of control, corporate culture, and employee resistance in general. In "Addition By Subtraction," *HR Magazine*, March 1995, pp. 38–43, James C. Spee provides an analysis on the importance of cooperative relationships. Brief yet valuable managerial tips are contained in Margaret Kaeter, "An Outsourcing Primer," *Training & Development*, November 1995, pp. 20–25; Len Marinaccio, "Outsourcing: A Strategic Tool For Managing Human Resources," *Employee Benefits Journal*, March 1994, pp. 39–42; Kathleen Correia, "Get Into The Outsourcing Loop," *HRFocus*, April 1994, p. 15; Kathleen Correia, "HR Enters The Outsourcing Loop," *Managing Office Technology*, September 1994, p. 37; and Edward G. Pringle, "The Advantages Of Benefits Outsourcing," *Risk Management*, July 1995, pp. 61–64.

The literature on managing the outsourcing venture in a context other than HR is more voluminous. In *Beyond The Information System Outsourcing Bandwagon* (Chichester, England: John

Wiley & Sons, 1995), pp. 211–215, Mary C. Lacity and Rudy Hirschheim briefly set forth some guidelines on managing the outsourcing decision. *See also* Mary C. Lacity, Leslie P. Willcocks, and David F. Feeny, "IT Outsourcing: Maximize Flexibility And Control," *Harvard Business Review*, May–June 1995, pp. 84–93 (setting forth similar guidelines). In "Employing Service Organizations And Contractors," *Supervision*, July 1995, pp. 8–11, W. H. Weiss focuses on the importance of communication and effective conflict resolution. Other articles containing managerial guidelines for outsourcing include Dick Dole and Lee Pinkard, "If You Outsource . . .," *Journal Of Business Strategy*, May–June 1993, pp. 55–56; Echo Montgomery Garrett, "Outsourcing To The Max," *Small Business Reports*, August 1994, pp. 9–14; and N. Dean Mayer, "A Sensible Approach To Outsourcing," *Information Systems Management*, Fall 1994, pp. 23–27. For accounts of how certain companies have managed their outsourcing relationships, *see* Joe Dysart, "JIT-II Rings Up Big Savings," *Distribution*, December 1993, pp. 45–47 (focusing on AT&T), and Chris Gillis, "Never Outsource Control," *American Shipper*, January 1995, pp. 28–30 (focusing on DuPont). For six varied opinions on how to resolve a outsourcing conflict set forth in a hypothetical case study, *see* Richard Peisch, "When Outsourcing Goes Awry," *Harvard Business Review*, May–June 1995, pp. 24–37 (also discussing the importance of selecting the right service provider and entering the right contract).

There are also many resources on managing strategic partnerships — an area which has broad, relevant application to managing the outsourcing of an HR service. Particularly noteworthy here is James Brian Quinn's groundbreaking work, *Intelligent Enterprise* (New York: The Free Press, 1992), which, among other things, contains lucid discourses on the potential loss of control over suppliers (*see* pp. 49–55, 78–79) and the key factors and management issues in partnering success (*see* pp. 384–395). *See also* James Brian Quinn and Frederick G. Hilmer, "Strategic Outsourcing," *Sloan Management Review*, Summer 1994, pp. 43–55. Another outstanding resource along these lines is David Limerick and Bert Cunnington, *Managing The New Organization* (San Francisco: Jossey-Bass Publishers, 1993), pp. 87–111.

For a theoretical discussion on how to build and structure your strategic partnerships, *see* Martha C. Cooper and John T. Gardner, "Building Good Business Relationships — More Than Just Partnering Or Strategic Alliances?," *International Journal Of Physical Distribution & Logistics Management*, Volume 23 Number 6 1993, pp. 14–26. For a case study on how one small company manages its strategic partnerships, *see* "How Virtual Corporations Manage The Performance Of Contractors: The Super Bakery Case," *Organizational Dynamics*, Summer 1995, pp. 70–75. Finally, for a compelling and incisive analysis of managing through trust, *see* Charles Handy, "Trust And The Virtual Organization," *Harvard Business Review*, May–June 1995, pp. 40–50.

Chapter Ten

Assessing, Measuring, and Evaluating Outsourcing

Although the literature in the field of assessment, measurement, and evaluation is voluminous, only a few human resource articles touch upon the issue within the context of outsourcing. In "Outsourcing Through Partnerships," *Training & Development*, October 1995, pp. 51–55, Garry J. DeRose and Janet McLaughlin indicate how Corning evaluated its outsourcing partnership with an external training vendor. For an article emphasizing the importance of benchmarking information within the context of the outsourcing decision, *see* James C. Spee, "Addition By Subtraction, " *HR Magazine*, March 1995, pp. 38–43. *See also* James Brian Quinn, *Intelligent Enterprise* (New York: The Free Press, 1992), pp. 93–96 (emphasizing the importance of benchmarking information within the context of the outsourcing decision), and Mary C. Lacity and Rudy Hirschheim, *Beyond The Information Systems Outsourcing Bandwagon* (Chichester, England: John Wiley & Sons, 1995), pp. 136–156 (examining the use of benchmarking within the context of information systems insourcing decisions).

As noted, the literature relating to the field of assessment, measurement, and evaluation is rich, indeed. Some of the best resources along these lines include Jac Fitz-enz, *How To Measure Human Resources Management* (New York: McGraw Hill, Inc., 1984); Donald L. Kirkpatrick, *Evaluating Training Programs* (San Francisco: Berrett-Koehler Publishers, 1994); and Wayne F. Cascio, *Costing Human Resources: The Financial Impact Of Behavior In Organizations* (Boston: PWS-Kent Publishing Company, 1991).